Recipe Collection

BAKING

Most Trusted Recipes

Publications International Ltd.

Favorite Brand Name Recipes at www.fbnr.com

Recipes developed and tested by Land O'Lakes Test Kitchens. For questions regarding recipes in this cookbook or LAND O LAKES® products, call: 1-800-328-4155

Pictured on the front cover: Raspberry Cheesecake with Chocolate Crust (*page 76*).

Pictured on the back cover : Chocolate Cake with Peanut Butter Frosting (*page 154*).

ISBN-13: 978-1-4127-2540-8
ISBN-10: 1-4127-2540-2

Manufactured in China.

8 7 6 5 4 3 2 1

Preparation and Cooking Times:
All recipes were developed and tested in the Land O'Lakes Test Kitchens by professional home economists. Use "Preparation Time" and "Cooking, Baking, Microwaving or Broiling Time" given with each recipe as guides. Preparation time is based on the approximate amount of "active" time required to assemble the recipe. This includes steps such as chopping, mixing, cooking pasta, frosting, etc. Cooking, baking, microwaving or broiling times are based on the minimum amount of time required for these recipe steps.

CONTENTS

36

87

126

BAKING

It's better with butter

Nothing equals the wonderful flavor of real butter and the homemade goodness it adds to baked goods. When you bake, butter plays a major role in tenderizing, adding flavor and color, and helping your baked goods to brown. Here are some tips for better baking with butter:

What is the best way to soften butter? Soften butter for easier mixing by removing it from the refrigerator and letting it stand 30 to 45 minutes at room temperature. In a hurry? Cut butter into chunks and let stand 15 minutes at room temperature, or place a stick of cold butter between sheets of waxed paper and hit it with a rolling pin on each side to smash butter. We don't recommend softening butter in the microwave because it can melt too quickly.

Can salted and unsalted butter be substituted for one another? Unsalted butter may be substituted for salted butter or vice versa. It is not necessary to alter the amount of salt in the recipe. Unsalted butter gives recipes a delicate, cultured flavor.

How long can I store my butter? Always refrigerate butter in its original wrapping, in its original package, and store in the coldest part of the refrigerator—not in the "butter keeper" in the door. Butter will retain its freshness for four months. For longer storage, freeze in the carton.

Measuring Tips

Butter: Cut the stick at the desired marking on the wrapper, using a sharp knife.

1 cup = 2 sticks = ½ pound

⅔ cup = 10 tablespoons plus 2 teaspoons

½ cup = 1 stick = ¼ pound

⅓ cup = 5 tablespoons plus 1 teaspoon

¼ cup = ½ stick = 4 tablespoons

Flour: Stir flour with a large spoon to loosen it up. Lightly spoon flour into a dry measuring cup and level top with a spatula or knife. Do not tap or shake the measuring cup when measuring, or you will get too much flour. Sifting isn't necessary unless the recipe specifically calls for it.

Brown sugar: Pack firmly into dry measuring cup until level with top.

Cornmeal, granulated sugar, oats, and powdered sugar: Spoon into a dry measuring cup and level top with a spatula or knife.

Leavenings and spices: Fill a standard measuring spoon to the top and level with a spatula or knife.

Liquids: A common baking mistake is measuring liquid ingredients in dry measuring cups. All liquids—including milk, honey, corn syrup—should be poured into a glass or clear plastic liquid measuring cup on a level surface. Bend down so your eye is level with the marking on the cup for an accurate reading. For easy removal of sticky liquids such as corn syrup, honey, or molasses, spray the measuring cup first with cooking spray.

For Best Results...

- Read through the entire recipe before you start to make sure you have all the necessary ingredients.

- Prepare ingredients that need to be softened, toasted, chopped, grated, or peeled first.
- Use dry measuring cups for dry ingredients and glass or clear plastic measuring cups for liquids.

The Basic Tools

The following is a list of pantry basics:

- Bread (loaf) pans 9×5×3 or 8×4×3-inch
- Cake pans (aluminum) 13×9-inch, 8- or 9-inch square, 12-cup Bundt®, or 10-inch tube pan
- Cookie and/or biscuit cutters
- Cookie sheets approximately 14×17-inch, shiny aluminum without sides
- Electric hand-held or stand-up mixer
- Wooden spoons
- Rubber spatula
- Kitchen timer
- 15×10×1-inch jelly-roll pan
- Measuring cups and spoons
- Metal spatula or turner
- Mixing bowls
- 12-cup muffin pan
- Rolling pin

Feta Cheesecake, p. 14
Blue Cheese Appetizer Tart *(opposite page)*, p. 18

BAKED
BITES

Whether you're feeding your family and friends or hosting a more formal occasion, part of entertaining your guests is providing something delectable and delightful to eat. These savory, oven-baked bites will help you serve fantastic first courses and delicious snacks that are sure to please.

Sweet & Savory Snack Mix

Preparation time: **10 minutes** | Baking time: **1 hour** | **8 cups**

3 cups pretzel sticks

3 cups honey graham cereal

2 cups crispy wheat cereal squares

1½ cups mixed nuts

½ cup LAND O LAKES® Butter, melted

3 tablespoons firmly packed brown sugar

2 tablespoons Worcestershire sauce

• Heat oven to 250°F. Combine pretzels, honey graham cereal, cereal squares and mixed nuts in ungreased 15×10×1-inch jelly-roll pan.

• Combine butter, brown sugar and Worcestershire sauce in small bowl. Pour over cereal mixture; toss lightly to coat.

• Bake, stirring every 15 minutes, for 1 hour. Cool completely. Store in container with tight-fitting lid.

Nutty Artichoke Spread

Preparation time: **20 minutes** | Baking time: **20 minutes** | 2½ cups

⅔ cup mayonnaise

½ cup finely chopped pecans

1 (8-ounce) package (2 cups)
   LAND O LAKES® Chedarella® or
   Cheddar Cheese, shredded

4 slices bacon, crisply cooked,
   crumbled

1 (14-ounce) can artichoke hearts,
   drained, quartered

1 tablespoon finely chopped onion

1 tablespoon lemon juice

   Sliced artisan bread or crackers

• Heat oven to 350°F. Stir together all ingredients except bread in large bowl. Spoon mixture into ungreased 9-inch ovenproof shallow dish or pie plate.

• Bake for 20 to 25 minutes or until cheese is melted and spread is heated through. Serve with sliced bread or crackers.

Sweet & Sour Meatballs

Preparation time: **15 minutes** | Baking time: **25 minutes** | **5 dozen meatballs**

Sauce

- 1 (20-ounce) can pineapple chunks in juice, drained, reserve juice
- 2 tablespoons LAND O LAKES® Butter
- 2 tablespoons firmly packed brown sugar
- 1 tablespoon cornstarch
- 2 tablespoons cider vinegar
- 1 tablespoon soy sauce
- ½ teaspoon ground ginger
- 2 medium green and/or red bell peppers, cut into 1-inch pieces

Meatballs

- 2 (1-pound) packages frozen pre-cooked meatballs, thawed

• Heat oven to 350°F. Combine reserved pineapple juice, butter, brown sugar, cornstarch, vinegar, soy sauce and ginger in 1-quart saucepan. Cook over medium heat, stirring occasionally, until mixture is thickened and bubbly (4 to 6 minutes). Boil, stirring constantly, 1 minute.

• Place sauce, pineapple chunks, bell peppers and meatballs in ungreased 2-quart casserole; stir gently to coat. Cover; bake for 25 to 30 minutes or until meatballs are heated through. Serve in chafing dish with toothpicks or keep warm in slow cooker.

Mushroom Pinwheels

Preparation time: **25 minutes** | Baking time: **15 minutes** | **60 pinwheels**

¼ cup LAND O LAKES® Butter

1 (8-ounce) package sliced fresh
   mushrooms, finely chopped

2 tablespoons all-purpose flour

¼ teaspoon salt

½ cup LAND O LAKES™ Half & Half

1 teaspoon finely chopped fresh dill

1 teaspoon lemon juice

½ teaspoon garlic or onion salt

20 slices soft sandwich bread

2 tablespoons LAND O LAKES®
   Butter, melted

Fresh dill, if desired

• Heat oven to 400°F. Melt ¼ cup butter in 12-inch skillet until sizzling; add mushrooms. Cook over medium-high heat until mushrooms are softened (about 5 minutes). Stir in flour and salt; mix until well blended. Add half & half; continue cooking, stirring constantly, until mixture is thickened. Stir in 1 teaspoon dill, lemon juice and garlic salt. Pour mushroom mixture into shallow dish. Cover with plastic food wrap; refrigerate until cool and thickened (about 30 minutes).

• Meanwhile, cut crusts from bread. Roll bread slices with rolling pin until very thin. Spread 1 tablespoon mushroom mixture on each slice; roll up. Place rolls onto parchment paper-lined or greased aluminum foil-lined baking sheets, seam-side down. Freeze for 15 minutes.

• Cut rolls into thirds using serrated knife; separate on baking sheets. Brush with melted butter. Bake for 15 to 17 minutes or until golden brown. Serve immediately. Garnish with fresh dill, if desired.

tip:
To make ahead, prepare as directed above except do not cut, brush with butter or bake. Wrap pinwheels in plastic food wrap; place in freezer bag. Freeze for up to 2 weeks. Thaw rolls at room temperature for 30 minutes before slicing. Heat oven to 400°F. Brush with butter and bake as directed above.

Maple-Glazed Beef Short Ribs

Preparation time: **30 minutes** | Cooking time: **55 minutes** | Grilling time: **20 minutes** | **6 servings**

Ribs

4 pounds beef short ribs

5 cups water

Glaze

¼ cup LAND O LAKES® Butter

1 medium (½ cup) onion, chopped

1 cup pure maple or maple-flavored syrup

½ cup apple cider

¼ cup soy sauce

2 tablespoons stone-ground mustard

½ teaspoon salt

• Combine ribs and water in 5-quart saucepan or Dutch oven. Cover; cook over medium heat, stirring occasionally, until water comes to a full boil (10 to 15 minutes). Reduce heat to low; cook until ribs are tender (30 to 35 minutes). Drain; pat dry.

• Meanwhile, heat one side of gas grill on medium or charcoal grill until coals are ash white. Place coals to one side in charcoal grill. Make aluminum foil drip pan; place opposite coals.

• Melt butter in 2-quart saucepan until sizzling; add onion. Cook over medium heat, stirring occasionally, until onion is softened (6 to 8 minutes). Stir in all remaining glaze ingredients. Continue cooking, stirring occasionally, until mixture comes to a full boil (6 to 8 minutes). Reduce heat to medium-low. Cook, stirring occasionally, until sauce thickens slightly and flavors blend (15 to 20 minutes). Reserve ½ cup glaze.

• Place ribs on grill over drip pan. Cover; grill, turning occasionally and brushing with reserved ½ cup glaze, until ribs are fork tender and heated through (20 to 25 minutes). Serve with remaining hot glaze.

tip:
Leftover glaze can also be used on chicken or pork. Brush glaze on during last 10 minutes of grilling.

tip:
Ribs are precooked to shorten grilling time and to tenderize meat.

Feta Cheesecake

Preparation time: **30 minutes** | Baking time: **35 minutes** | **32 servings**

Crust

1⅓ cups (about 35) sesame seed cracker crumbs

¼ cup shredded Parmesan cheese

⅓ cup LAND O LAKES® Butter, melted

Filling

2 (8-ounce) packages cream cheese, softened

2 (4-ounce) packages crumbled feta cheese with basil and tomato

3 eggs

1 (4¼-ounce) can (½ cup) chopped pitted ripe olives, well-drained

⅓ cup sliced green onions

1 teaspoon dried oregano leaves

½ teaspoon coarse ground pepper

¼ teaspoon garlic salt

Topping

2 medium Roma tomatoes, finely chopped

⅓ cup sliced green onions

Sesame seed or rye crackers, if desired

• Heat oven to 325°F. Combine all crust ingredients in medium bowl. Press onto bottom and 1½-inches up sides of ungreased 9-inch springform pan or aluminum foil-lined 9-inch round baking pan, leaving a 1-inch overhang.

• Combine cream cheese and feta cheese in large bowl. Beat at medium speed, scraping bowl often, until creamy. Add eggs, beating just until combined. Stir in all remaining filling ingredients. Pour into crust. Bake for 35 to 40 minutes or until just set 3 inches from edge of pan. Cool 15 minutes; loosen sides of springform pan. Cool on wire rack for 2 hours. Loosely cover; refrigerate at least 2 hours.

• To serve, cut into wedges. Top each wedge with tomato and green onions. Serve with crackers, if desired. Store refrigerated.

tip:

Check cheesecakes at the minimum time for doneness by gently shaking the pan. If the center still jiggles and the edges appear firm, the cheesecake is done. The cheesecake will continue to set as it cools.

Melt-In-Your-Mouth Herbed Shortbread

Preparation time: **10 minutes** | Baking time: **32 minutes** | **9 servings**

1 cup all-purpose flour

½ cup LAND O LAKES® Butter, softened

2 ounces (½ cup) LAND O LAKES® Cheddar Cheese, shredded

½ teaspoon dried basil leaves

¼ teaspoon dried thyme leaves

¼ teaspoon ground mustard

⅛ teaspoon garlic powder

⅛ teaspoon coarse ground pepper

• Heat oven to 350°F. Combine all ingredients in large bowl. Beat at medium speed just until soft dough forms.

• Press dough evenly onto bottom of ungreased 8-inch square baking pan. Bake for 32 to 37 minutes until golden brown. Cool 5 minutes in pan on cooling rack. While still warm, carefully cut into squares. Cool completely.

tip:

For appetizer servings, cut each square in half diagonally.

Indian-Spiced Chicken Wings

Preparation time: **10 minutes** | Baking time: **30 minutes** | 24 drummettes, 1 cup chutney

4 teaspoons curry powder

2 teaspoons ground ginger

1 teaspoon ground cinnamon

¼ teaspoon salt

2 pounds (24) chicken wing drummettes

3 tablespoons LAND O LAKES® Butter, melted

1 cup mango chutney

• Place curry powder, ginger, cinnamon and salt in large resealable plastic food storage bag. Add chicken; seal. Shake bag until chicken is evenly coated with spices. Refrigerate for at least 3 hours or overnight.

• Heat oven to 350°F. Arrange chicken on aluminum foil-lined 15×10×1-inch jelly-roll pan. Drizzle with butter. Bake for 30 to 35 minutes or until chicken is golden brown and crisp and juices run clear when pierced with a fork.

• Serve chicken with chutney.

tip:
Look for a variety of chutney flavors at the supermarket. Mango chutney is the most classic, but apple, peach and ginger chutneys would be equally delicious with the chicken.

Blue Cheese Appetizer Tart *(photo on page 7)*

Preparation time: **30 minutes** | Baking time: **37 minutes** | **16 servings**

Pastry

1½ cups all-purpose flour

½ cup cold LAND O LAKES® Butter

5 to 6 tablespoons cold water

Filling

1 (8-ounce) package cream cheese, softened

⅓ cup crumbled blue cheese

¼ cup LAND O LAKES™ Heavy Whipping Cream

1 egg, slightly beaten

¼ teaspoon coarse ground pepper

⅓ cup chopped roasted red bell peppers

3 tablespoons lightly toasted pine nuts or your favorite chopped nuts

2 tablespoons chopped fresh parsley

• Heat oven to 375°F. Place flour in large bowl; cut in butter with pastry blender or fork until mixture resembles coarse crumbs. Stir in enough cold water with fork until flour mixture is just moistened. Shape into ball.

• Roll out pastry on lightly floured surface to 12-inch circle. Place into ungreased 9- or 10-inch tart pan with removable bottom or pie pan. Press firmly on bottom and up sides of pan. Cut away excess pastry; prick all over with fork. Bake for 17 to 22 minutes or until very lightly browned.

• Meanwhile, combine cream cheese and blue cheese in large bowl. Beat at medium speed, scraping bowl often, until creamy. Continue beating, gradually adding whipping cream, egg and ground pepper until blended. Spread into baked pastry shell. Sprinkle with roasted red pepper, pine nuts and parsley.

• Bake for 20 to 25 minutes or until filling is set. Let stand 20 minutes before serving. To serve, cut into wedges. Cover; store refrigerated.

tip:

To toast pine nuts, spread evenly on shallow baking pan. Bake at 325°F. for 5 to 7 minutes, stirring occasionally, just until lightly browned.

Tomato & Roasted Garlic Tart

Preparation time: **25 minutes** | Baking time: **58 minutes** | **12 servings**

1 large garlic bulb

1 teaspoon olive oil

1 sheet frozen puff pastry, thawed

4 medium (2 cups) Roma tomatoes, thinly sliced

¼ teaspoon salt

5 ounces (1¼ cups) LAND O LAKES® Chedarella® Cheese, finely shredded

½ teaspoon dried basil leaves, crushed

¼ teaspoon freshly ground pepper

• Heat oven to 375°F. Slice top off garlic bulb, exposing cloves. Place onto large piece of aluminum foil; drizzle with olive oil. Fold aluminum foil over garlic to seal. Place onto ungreased small baking sheet. Bake for 45 to 50 minutes or until garlic is very tender. Remove from oven; cool completely.

• Meanwhile, line another baking sheet with parchment paper. Roll out puff pastry on parchment paper-lined baking sheet into 11-inch square. Pinch pastry to form ¼-inch edge. Prick bottom with fork; cover with plastic food wrap. Refrigerate for 30 minutes.

• Lightly sprinkle tomatoes with salt; place onto paper towels to remove excess moisture. Pat dry.

• Increase oven temperature to 425°F. Squeeze roasted garlic from skins into small bowl; mash with fork. Spread over bottom of pastry. Top with ¾ cup cheese. Arrange tomatoes in rows on top of cheese; sprinkle with basil and pepper. Top with remaining cheese. Bake for 13 to 16 minutes or until pastry is golden brown and cheese is melted.

tip:
To save time in preparing this tart, bake the garlic the day before and refrigerate until ready to use.

Cheddar Shortbread Bites

Preparation time: **20 minutes** | Baking time: **12 minutes** | **60 appetizers**

Shortbread

1 cup all-purpose flour

½ cup LAND O LAKES® Butter, softened

½ teaspoon salt

Dash ground red pepper

8 ounces (2 cups) LAND O LAKES® Sharp Cheddar Cheese, shredded

Topping

2 tablespoons poppy seed

2 tablespoons sesame seed

1 egg white

1 tablespoon water

• Combine flour, butter, salt and red pepper in medium bowl; beat at medium speed until dough forms. Add cheese; mix until ball forms. Shape dough into 8-inch ball; flatten slightly. Wrap in plastic food wrap; refrigerate 2 hours or overnight.

• Heat oven to 350°F. Roll out dough on lightly floured surface to ¼-inch thickness. (It will be hard to roll at first, but will soften. Press together any cracks that form on edges of dough.) Cut dough with 1½-inch cookie cutters or pizza cutter into desired shapes (squares, triangles, circles). Place onto ungreased baking sheets.

• Combine poppy seed and sesame seed in small bowl. Beat egg white and water in another small bowl. Brush cut-outs with egg white mixture; sprinkle with seed mixture.

• Bake for 12 to 15 minutes or until very lightly browned around edges. Immediately loosen from baking sheets; cool on baking sheets.

tip:

Lining baking sheets with kitchen parchment paper makes shortbread easier to remove and clean-up faster.

tip:

Shortbread can be topped with a variety of other ingredients, such as chili powder, seasoned salt, fennel seed or herbs.

Pear & Gorgonzola Focaccia

Preparation time: **25 minutes** | Baking time: **17 minutes** | 12 wedges

1 (1-pound) loaf frozen white bread dough, thawed

3 tablespoons LAND O LAKES® Butter, melted

1 large (1½ cups) ripe pear, cored, sliced*

1 tablespoon sugar

⅓ cup chopped red bell pepper

1 tablespoon chopped fresh rosemary

4 ounces Gorgonzola or blue cheese, crumbled

• Grease 12-inch pizza pan. Press bread dough into prepared pan, forming a ridge around edge of pan. Brush with 1 tablespoon butter. Let rise in warm place until double in size (20 minutes).

• Meanwhile, melt remaining butter in heavy 10-inch skillet until sizzling; add pear slices. Cook over medium heat 3 minutes, gently turning occasionally. Sprinkle with sugar. Continue cooking until pears are tender (4 to 6 minutes).

• Heat oven to 400°F. Place pears over dough; sprinkle with red pepper and rosemary. Bake for 15 to 20 minutes or until crust is deep golden brown. Sprinkle with Gorgonzola; continue baking until cheese begins to melt (2 to 3 minutes). Serve hot or warm.

*Substitute 1 large (1½ cups) apple, cored, sliced.

tip:

Gorgonzola is Italy's version of blue cheese, made with cow's milk. The cheese is inoculated with Penicillium mold to create the blue-green veins in a creamy, golden cheese. When it is young, Gorgonzola is creamy and smooth, but becomes sharper in flavor and drier in texture as it ages.

Orange Coconut Muffins, p. 32

Artichoke-Olive Focaccia
(opposite page), p. 36

BREAD
& BUTTER

Few things taste better than a slice of freshly baked bread, still warm from the oven and topped with a pat of sweet butter. Whether you use the following recipes to bake up a batch of buttermilk biscuits or put together a rustic focaccia, you're sure to satisfy the whole gang.

Spiced Pear Bread

Preparation time: **20 minutes** | Baking time: **50 minutes** | **16 servings (1 loaf)**

Bread

¾ cup sugar

½ cup LAND O LAKES® Butter, softened

2 eggs

2 tablespoons pear nectar or orange juice

½ teaspoon vanilla

1¼ cups (about 1 large) shredded ripe pear, unpeeled

1¾ cups all-purpose flour

1½ teaspoons ground cinnamon

1¼ teaspoons baking powder

1 teaspoon ground ginger

½ teaspoon salt

½ teaspoon baking soda

⅓ cup chopped walnuts

Glaze

½ cup powdered sugar

1 to 2 tablespoons pear nectar or orange juice

• Heat oven to 350°F. Combine sugar and butter in large bowl. Beat at medium speed, scraping bowl often, until creamy. Add eggs, pear nectar and vanilla; continue beating until well mixed. Add shredded pear; continue beating until combined. Reduce speed to low. Add all remaining bread ingredients except walnuts; beat just until blended. Stir in walnuts by hand.

• Spoon batter into greased 9x5-inch loaf pan. Bake for 50 to 60 minutes or until toothpick inserted in center comes out clean. Let stand 10 minutes; remove from pan. Cool completely.

• Combine all glaze ingredients in small bowl. Drizzle over loaf.

tip:

For gift giving, make 3 mini loaves instead of one large loaf. Prepare batter as directed above. Spoon into 3 greased (5½×3-inch) mini loaf pans or aluminum foil pans. Bake for 35 to 40 minutes or until toothpick inserted in center comes out clean. Glaze mini loaves as directed above.

Golden Pumpkin Bread

Preparation time: **15 minutes** | Baking time: **30 minutes** | **24 servings (3 mini loaves)**

1½	cups all-purpose flour
1	cup firmly packed brown sugar
1	cup canned pumpkin
½	cup LAND O LAKES® Butter, softened
2	eggs
1½	teaspoons ground cinnamon
1	teaspoon baking powder
1	teaspoon baking soda
1	teaspoon salt
½	teaspoon ground ginger
¼	teaspoon ground cloves

• Heat oven to 350°F. Combine all ingredients in large bowl. Beat at medium speed, scraping bowl often, until well mixed.

• Spoon into 3 greased mini (5½×3-inch) loaf pans. Bake for 30 to 35 minutes or until toothpick inserted in center comes out clean. Cool 10 minutes; remove from pan. Cool completely. Store refrigerated.

tip:
Bread can be baked in greased 9×5-inch loaf pan. Bake for 45 to 55 minutes or until toothpick inserted in center comes out clean.

Rhubarb Streusel Bread

Preparation time: **40 minutes** | Baking time: **1 hour 5 minutes** | **12 servings (1 loaf)**

Bread

- 1 cup sugar
- ½ cup LAND O LAKES® Butter, softened
- ⅓ cup orange juice
- 2 eggs
- 2 cups all-purpose flour
- 1 teaspoon baking powder
- ¼ teaspoon baking soda
- ¼ teaspoon salt
- 1½ cups (¼-inch) sliced fresh rhubarb*

Streusel

- 2 tablespoons sugar
- 2 tablespoons firmly packed brown sugar
- 1 tablespoon all-purpose flour
- 1 tablespoon LAND O LAKES® Butter, melted
- 1½ teaspoons ground cinnamon

• Heat oven to 350°F. Grease and flour 8×4-inch loaf pan.

• Combine 1 cup sugar and ½ cup butter in large bowl. Beat at medium speed, scraping bowl often, until creamy. Reduce speed to low; add orange juice and eggs. Continue beating just until mixed. (Mixture will look slightly curdled.) Stir in flour, baking powder, baking soda and salt by hand just until moistened. Gently stir in rhubarb. (Batter will be thick.)

• Reserve 1½ cups batter. Spread remaining batter into prepared pan. Combine all streusel ingredients in small bowl; stir until mixture resembles coarse crumbs. Sprinkle half of streusel over batter in pan; gently press into batter. Carefully spread reserved batter into pan; top with remaining streusel. Press streusel into batter.

• Bake for 65 to 70 minutes or until toothpick inserted in center comes out clean. Cool 10 minutes; remove from pan.

*Substitute 1½ cups frozen rhubarb, thawed.

tip:
Bread can be prepared in greased and floured 9×5-inch loaf pan. Bake for 60 to 65 minutes.

tip:
This is a great make-ahead bread as the flavors are almost better the second day. Once loaf is completely cooled, wrap in aluminum foil and refrigerate. This bread also freezes well.

Nutmeg Streusel Muffins

Preparation time: **10 minutes** | Baking time: **18 minutes** | **1 dozen muffins**

Streusel

- 1⅓ cups all-purpose flour
- 1 cup firmly packed brown sugar
- ½ cup cold LAND O LAKES® Butter

Muffins

- ⅔ cup all-purpose flour
- ⅔ cup buttermilk*
- 1 egg
- 1½ teaspoons baking powder
- 1½ teaspoons ground nutmeg
- ½ teaspoon baking soda
- ½ teaspoon salt

• Heat oven to 400°F. Combine 1⅓ cups flour and brown sugar in large bowl; cut in butter with pastry blender or fork until mixture resembles coarse crumbs. Reserve ½ cup.

• Add all muffin ingredients to remaining streusel mixture in same bowl; stir just until moistened.

• Spoon batter into greased or paper-lined 12-cup muffin pan. Sprinkle each with reserved streusel. Bake for 18 to 22 minutes or until lightly browned. Let stand 5 minutes; remove from pan.

*Substitute 2 teaspoons vinegar or lemon juice and enough milk to equal ⅔ cup. Let stand 10 minutes.

Southern Skillet Cornbread

Preparation time: **15 minutes** | Baking time: **15 minutes** | 9 servings

1 cup all-purpose flour

1 cup white or yellow cornmeal

1 tablespoon sugar

2 teaspoons baking powder

1 teaspoon baking soda

¼ teaspoon salt

1 cup buttermilk*

⅓ cup LAND O LAKES® Butter, melted

2 eggs, beaten

1 tablespoon LAND O LAKES® Butter

• Heat oven to 400°F. Combine flour, cornmeal, sugar, baking powder, baking soda and salt in medium bowl. Stir in buttermilk, ⅓ cup melted butter and eggs just until flour mixture is moistened.

• Melt 1 tablespoon butter in heavy cast iron or oven-proof 10-inch skillet (2 to 4 minutes). Immediately pour batter into pan. Bake for 15 to 20 minutes or until toothpick inserted in center comes out clean. Serve warm.

*Substitute 1 tablespoon vinegar or lemon juice and enough milk to equal 1 cup. Let stand 10 minutes.

Coconut Cherry Scones with Citrus Butter

Preparation time: **20 minutes** | Baking time: **20 minutes** | 8 scones; ½ cup citrus butter

Butter

- ½ cup LAND O LAKES® Butter, softened
- 1 tablespoon powdered sugar
- 1 teaspoon freshly grated lemon peel
- 1 teaspoon freshly grated orange peel

Scones

- 2 cups all-purpose flour
- ¼ cup sugar
- 2½ teaspoons baking powder
- ¼ teaspoon salt
- ½ cup cold LAND O LAKES® Butter
- 1 egg, beaten
- ½ cup LAND O LAKES™ Half & Half
- ⅓ cup sweetened flaked coconut
- ½ cup dried cherries or sweetened dried cranberries, chopped
- 1 teaspoon freshly grated lemon peel
- 1 tablespoon coarse grain or decorator sugar

• Heat oven to 375°F. Combine all butter ingredients in small bowl. Beat at low speed, scraping bowl often, until creamy. Set aside.

• Combine flour, sugar, baking powder and salt in medium bowl; cut in ½ cup butter with pastry blender or fork until mixture resembles coarse crumbs. Combine egg, half & half, coconut, cherries and lemon peel in small bowl. Add to flour mixture. Stir just until flour mixture is moistened.

• Turn dough onto lightly floured surface; knead lightly 8 to 10 times. Pat dough into 7-inch circle. Place onto greased baking sheet. Cut into 8 wedges. (Do not separate.) Sprinkle with coarse sugar. Bake for 20 to 25 minutes or until golden brown. Cool 15 minutes. Cut wedges apart; remove from baking sheet. Serve warm scones with citrus butter.

tip:

Scotland takes the credit for developing scones, although the British have made them popular all over the world. This biscuit-like quick bread derived its name from the Stone of Destiny (or Scone) where Scottish kings were once crowned.

Pepper Popovers with Sage Butter

Preparation time: **30 minutes** | Baking time: **35 minutes** | 6 popovers; ½ cup sage butter

Sage Butter

½ cup LAND O LAKES® Butter, softened

1½ teaspoons finely chopped fresh sage leaves*

¼ teaspoon coarse ground pepper

Popovers

3 eggs

1¼ cups milk

1¼ cups all-purpose flour

1½ teaspoons finely chopped fresh sage leaves*

¼ teaspoon coarse ground pepper

¼ teaspoon salt

• Heat oven to 400°F. Place all sage butter ingredients in small bowl. Beat at low speed, scraping bowl often, until creamy. Cover; refrigerate until serving time.

• Beat eggs in small bowl at medium speed, scraping bowl often, until thick and lemon-colored. Add all remaining ingredients; continue beating 1 minute.

• Pour batter into well-greased 6-cup popover pan or 6 (6-ounce) custard cups. Bake for 35 to 40 minutes or until golden brown. (DO NOT OPEN OVEN DOOR DURING BAKING.)

• Immediately prick popovers with fork to allow steam to escape; remove from pan. Serve warm with sage butter.

*Substitute ½ teaspoon dried sage leaves.

tip:

For best results, eggs and milk should be at room temperature.

Orange Coconut Muffins *(photo on page 22)*

Preparation time: **25 minutes** | Baking time: **18 minutes** | **1 dozen muffins**

Muffin

⅓ cup orange juice

¼ cup LAND O LAKES® Butter, melted

1 egg

1½ cups all-purpose flour

¼ cup sugar

1½ teaspoons baking powder

½ teaspoon baking soda

½ teaspoon salt

1 (11-ounce) can mandarin orange segments, drained

Topping

⅓ cup sweetened flaked coconut

¼ cup sugar

1 tablespoon LAND O LAKES® Butter, softened

½ teaspoon freshly grated orange peel

• Heat oven to 375°F. Combine orange juice, ¼ cup melted butter and egg in large bowl. Add all remaining muffin ingredients except orange segments; stir just until moistened. Gently stir in orange segments. Spoon batter into 12 paper-lined or greased muffin cups.

• Combine all topping ingredients in small bowl; sprinkle evenly over muffins. Bake for 18 to 23 minutes or until lightly browned. Let stand 5 minutes; remove from pan.

Perfect Buttermilk Biscuits

Preparation time: **15 minutes** | Baking time: **10 minutes** | **8 biscuits**

2 cups all-purpose flour

2 teaspoons baking powder

¼ teaspoon baking soda

¼ teaspoon salt

½ cup cold LAND O LAKES® Butter

¾ cup buttermilk*

1 tablespoon LAND O LAKES® Butter, melted

• Heat oven to 450°F. Combine flour, baking powder, baking soda and salt in large bowl; cut in ½ cup butter with pastry blender or fork until mixture resembles coarse crumbs. Stir in buttermilk just until flour is moistened.

• Turn dough onto lightly floured surface; knead about 10 times or until smooth. Roll out dough to ¾-inch thickness. Cut into biscuits with 2½-inch biscuit cutter.

• Place biscuits 1 inch apart onto ungreased baking sheet. Brush biscuits with melted butter. Bake for 10 to 14 minutes or until lightly browned. Serve warm.

*Substitute 1 tablespoon vinegar or lemon juice plus enough milk to equal ¾ cup. Let stand 10 minutes.

variations:

Savory Herb Biscuits: Omit salt. Add ¼ to ½ teaspoon garlic salt and 1 tablespoon fresh or 1 teaspoon dried herbs (dill weed, chives or crushed rosemary leaves). Bake as directed.

Cinnamon Raisin Biscuits: Omit salt. Add 2 tablespoons sugar and ¾ teaspoon ground cinnamon with flour. Stir in ⅓ cup raisins with buttermilk. Brush with melted butter and sprinkle biscuits with sugar before baking. Bake as directed.

Drop Biscuits: Use 1¼ cups buttermilk. Drop dough by ¼ cupfuls onto lightly greased baking sheet. Do not brush biscuits with melted butter. Bake for 10 to 12 minutes.

Prize-Winning Blueberry Muffins

Preparation time: **20 minutes** | Baking time: **20 minutes** | **1 dozen muffins**

½ cup sugar	1½ cups all-purpose flour
¼ cup LAND O LAKES® Butter, softened	1 teaspoon baking soda
1 cup LAND O LAKES® Sour Cream	1 cup fresh or frozen (do not thaw) blueberries
1 egg	
1 tablespoon lemon juice	1 tablespoon sugar
1 teaspoon freshly grated lemon peel	½ teaspoon freshly grated lemon peel

• Heat oven to 375°F. Combine ½ cup sugar and butter in large bowl. Beat at medium speed, scraping bowl often, until creamy. Add sour cream, egg, lemon juice and 1 teaspoon lemon peel. Continue beating, scraping bowl often, until well mixed.

• Combine flour and baking soda in medium bowl. Stir flour mixture into sour cream mixture by hand just until moistened. Gently stir in blueberries. Spoon into greased or paper-lined 12-cup muffin pan.

• Combine 1 tablespoon sugar and ½ teaspoon lemon peel in small bowl. Sprinkle about ¼ teaspoon mixture on top of each muffin. Bake for 20 to 25 minutes or until lightly browned. Cool 5 minutes; remove from pan.

Flax Seed Cracker Bread

Preparation time: **20 minutes** | Baking time: **12 minutes** | **5½ dozen pieces**

1 cup whole wheat flour	½ teaspoon salt
½ cup all-purpose flour	¼ cup LAND O LAKES® Butter, softened
2 tablespoons sugar	½ cup buttermilk*
1 teaspoon baking powder	3 tablespoons flax seed or sesame seed
½ teaspoon baking soda	

• Heat oven to 375°F. Combine whole wheat flour, flour, sugar, baking powder, baking soda and salt in large bowl. Cut in butter with pastry blender or fork just until mixture resembles coarse crumbs. Add buttermilk; stir just until flour is moistened. Stir in flax seed.

• Place dough on lightly floured surface; knead 3 to 5 times until smooth. Divide dough in half. Roll out each half with floured rolling pin or pat each half with floured fingers into 13×11-inch rectangle on greased baking sheets. Prick all over with fork.

• Bake for 12 to 15 minutes or until golden brown. Cool completely. Break into pieces.

*Substitute 1½ teaspoons vinegar or lemon juice and enough milk to equal ½ cup. Let stand 10 minutes.

tip:
Varying shades of brown are typical of cracker bread. Try to roll or press dough out very evenly for even browning.

tip:
Flax seeds, when used as whole seeds, add texture to foods. Ground seeds give the most nutritional benefit and are a primary source of omega-3 and omega-6 fatty acids.

Basil Tomato Bread

Preparation time: **20 minutes** | Baking time: **30 minutes** | 16 servings; ½ cup butter

Butter

- ½ cup LAND O LAKES® Butter, softened
- 2 tablespoons grated Parmesan cheese
- 1 teaspoon Italian seasoning*

Bread

- 2½ cups all-purpose flour
- ⅓ cup grated Parmesan cheese
- 1 tablespoon sugar
- 2 teaspoons instant minced onion
- 1 teaspoon baking soda
- 1 teaspoon dried basil leaves
- ½ teaspoon salt
- 1 cup LAND O LAKES® Sour Cream
- ⅓ cup milk
- ⅓ cup chopped sun-dried tomatoes in oil
- ¼ cup LAND O LAKES® Butter, melted

Topping

- 1 egg white, slightly beaten
- 2 tablespoons grated Parmesan cheese

• Heat oven to 350°F. Combine all butter ingredients in small bowl. Beat at low speed, scraping bowl often, until creamy. Set aside.

• Combine flour, ⅓ cup Parmesan cheese, sugar, onion, baking soda, basil and salt in large bowl. Stir in sour cream, milk, tomatoes and ¼ cup melted butter just until moistened. Turn dough onto lightly floured surface; knead about 10 times or until smooth. Divide dough in half. Pat each half into 4½-inch round loaf.

• Place loaves 3 inches apart onto greased baking sheet. Brush tops with egg white. Sprinkle with 2 tablespoons Parmesan cheese. Cut an "X" about ½-inch deep in top of each loaf. Bake for 30 to 35 minutes or until golden brown. Remove from baking sheet; cool completely. Serve with prepared butter.

*Substitute ¼ teaspoon dried basil leaves, ¼ teaspoon dried marjoram leaves, ¼ teaspoon dried oregano leaves and ⅛ teaspoon dried sage.

Artichoke-Olive Focaccia

Preparation time: **1 hour** | Baking time: **30 minutes** | **12 servings**

Bread

- 3 to 3½ cups all-purpose or bread flour
- 1 (¼-ounce) package active dry yeast
- 1 tablespoon sugar
- 1 teaspoon salt
- 1 cup water
- 3 tablespoons LAND O LAKES® Butter
- 2 teaspoons finely chopped fresh garlic

Topping

- 1 tablespoon LAND O LAKES® Butter, melted
- 1 (6-ounce) jar marinated artichoke hearts, drained, cut large pieces in half
- ¼ cup sliced ripe olives
- ¼ cup roasted red pepper strips
- ½ cup shredded Parmesan cheese
- LAND O LAKES® Butter, melted, if desired

• Combine 1½ cups flour, yeast, sugar and salt in large bowl. Set aside.

• Combine water, 3 tablespoons butter and garlic in 1-quart saucepan. Cook over medium heat, stirring occasionally, until mixture reaches 120° to 130°F (2 to 4 minutes). (Butter may not melt completely.) Add warm butter mixture to flour mixture. Beat at low speed until flour is moistened. Increase speed to medium; beat, scraping bowl often, until smooth. Stir in enough remaining flour by hand until dough forms a ball and leaves sides of bowl.

• Turn dough onto lightly floured surface; knead until smooth and elastic (3 to 5 minutes), adding more flour as needed to prevent sticking.

• Press dough into 10-inch circle on greased baking sheet. Cover loosely with plastic food wrap; let rise in warm place until double in size (45 to 60 minutes).

• Heat oven to 375°F. Make indentations (about 1 inch deep) 2 inches apart in dough with floured finger or handle of wooden spoon. Brush dough with 1 tablespoon melted butter. Sprinkle artichokes, olives, red pepper strips and Parmesan cheese evenly over dough; press large pieces into dough.

• Bake for 30 to 35 minutes or until edges are golden brown. Brush with melted butter, if desired. Cut into wedges. Serve warm or cool.

BREAD MACHINE DIRECTIONS:

Place 3 cups all-purpose flour, 1½ teaspoons bread machine yeast, 1 tablespoon sugar, 1 teaspoon salt, 1 cup plus 3 tablespoons water, 3 tablespoons LAND O LAKES® Butter, softened and 2 teaspoons finely chopped fresh garlic in bread machine according to manufacturer's directions for DOUGH cycle. Shape dough and let rise as directed in recipe (30 to 40 minutes). Prepare topping and bake as directed in recipe.

Chewy Sourdough Breadsticks

Preparation time: **1 hour** | Baking time: **20 minutes** | **16 breadsticks**

Bread

4 to 4½ cups all-purpose flour or bread flour

2 tablespoons sugar

1 (¼-ounce) package active dry yeast

1 teaspoon salt

1 cup water

1 (6-ounce) carton (¾ cup) plain yogurt

2 tablespoons LAND O LAKES® Butter

2 tablespoons vinegar

Topping

1 egg white, slightly beaten

Sesame seed or poppy seed, if desired

Grated Parmesan cheese, if desired

Coarse salt, if desired

• Combine 1½ cups flour, sugar, yeast and salt in large bowl. Set aside.

• Combine water, yogurt and butter in 1-quart saucepan. Cook over medium heat, stirring occasionally, until mixture reaches 120° to 130°F (2 to 4 minutes). (Butter may not melt completely.) Add warm yogurt mixture and vinegar to flour mixture. Beat at medium speed, scraping bowl often, until smooth. Stir in enough remaining flour to make dough easy to handle.

• Turn dough onto lightly floured surface; knead until smooth and elastic (3 to 5 minutes). Invert large bowl over dough; let rise in warm place until almost double in size (30 to 60 minutes).

• Divide dough in half; roll each half into 10x8-inch rectangle. Cut each into 8 (1-inch wide) strips. Stretch each strip to about 12 inches long. Fold strip in half; twist several times. Pinch ends to seal. Place onto greased baking sheet. Cover loosely with plastic food wrap; let rise in warm place until double in size (15 to 20 minutes).

• Heat oven to 375°F. Brush breadsticks with beaten egg white. Sprinkle with desired topping. Bake for 20 to 25 minutes or until golden brown. Serve warm or cool.

tip:

Sourdough originally had to be made with a fermented "starter" to get its distinctive tangy flavor. Today, we can use other products to get a similar flavor without the lengthy procedure of making and keeping a starter.

Lemon Cornmeal Scones

Preparation time: **15 minutes** | Baking time: **15 minutes** | 8 scones

Topping

- 2 tablespoons sugar
- 1 teaspoon freshly grated lemon peel

Scones

- 1½ cups all-purpose flour
- ½ cup yellow cornmeal
- 2 tablespoons sugar
- 4 teaspoons baking powder
- ½ teaspoon salt
- 6 tablespoons cold LAND O LAKES® Butter, cut into 6 pieces
- ⅓ cup LAND O LAKES™ Half & Half
- 2 eggs
- 2 teaspoons freshly grated lemon peel

• Heat oven to 400°F. Combine all topping ingredients in small bowl; set aside.

• Combine flour, cornmeal, 2 tablespoons sugar, baking powder and salt in large bowl; cut in butter with pastry blender until mixture resembles coarse crumbs. (Particles should be the size of small peas.)

• Combine half & half, eggs and 2 teaspoons lemon peel in small bowl. Stir into flour mixture just until moistened. Knead dough on lightly floured surface 5 to 8 times until smooth, adding only enough flour as necessary to keep dough from sticking to surface.

• Pat dough into 9-inch circle on greased baking sheet. Sprinkle topping evenly over dough. Cut circle into 8 wedges with sharp knife, cutting almost all the way through. (DO NOT SEPARATE WEDGES.)

• Bake for 15 to 20 minutes or until lightly browned. Cool 10 minutes. Carefully separate scones.

variation:
Prepare scones as directed above, stirring in ½ cup sweetened dried cranberries, chopped dried apricots or chopped pecans after stirring in flour.

Flavored Butters

Pesto Cheese Butter

Preparation time: **5 minutes** | **½ cup**

- ½ cup LAND O LAKES® Butter, softened
- 1 tablespoon prepared pesto
- 1 tablespoon grated Parmesan cheese

• Combine all ingredients in small bowl; beat at medium speed until smooth.

• Store refrigerated in container with tight-fitting lid up to 2 weeks.

• Serve with warm artisan breads or tossed in hot cooked rotini, ziti or penne pasta.

Orange Cinnamon Butter

Preparation time: **5 minutes** | **½ cup**

- ½ cup LAND O LAKES® Butter, softened
- 1 tablespoon firmly packed brown sugar
- 1 teaspoon freshly grated orange peel
- ½ teaspoon ground cinnamon

• Combine all ingredients in small bowl; beat at medium speed until smooth.

• Store refrigerated in container with tight-fitting lid up to 2 weeks.

Southwestern Butter

Preparation time: **5 minutes** | **½ cup**

- ½ cup LAND O LAKES® Butter, softened
- 1 tablespoon salsa
- 1 tablespoon chopped fresh cilantro

• Combine all ingredients in small bowl; beat at medium speed until smooth.

• Store refrigerated in container with tight-fitting lid up to 2 weeks.

Sweet Maple Spread

Preparation time: **5 minutes** | **½ cup**

- ½ cup LAND O LAKES® Butter, softened
- 1 tablespoon maple-flavored syrup
- ¼ teaspoon maple flavor

• Combine all ingredients in small bowl; beat at medium speed until smooth.

• Store refrigerated in container with tight-fitting lid up to 2 weeks.

Berry Delicious Brownies, p. 56

Latte Cheesecake Bars
(opposite page), p. 58

BROWNIES
& BARS

Bake a panful of these sweet treats and watch your family come running. Fortunately, these delicious desserts are as easy to make as they are to eat!

Irish Mist Brownies

Preparation time: **30 minutes** | Baking time: **25 minutes** | **25 brownies**

Brownie

- ½ cup LAND O LAKES® Butter
- 2 (1-ounce) squares unsweetened baking chocolate
- 1 cup sugar
- ¾ cup all-purpose flour
- 2 eggs

Frosting

- 2 cups powdered sugar
- 1 (3-ounce) package cream cheese, softened
- 3 tablespoons LAND O LAKES® Butter, softened
- ½ teaspoon peppermint extract
- 2 to 3 drops green food color

Drizzle

- 1 (1-ounce) square unsweetened baking chocolate, melted

• Heat oven to 350°F. Melt ½ cup butter and 2 squares chocolate in 2-quart saucepan over medium heat, stirring constantly, until smooth (4 to 6 minutes). Stir in all remaining brownie ingredients until well mixed. Spread into greased 8-inch square baking pan.

• Bake for 25 to 30 minutes or until brownie begins to pull away from sides of pan. Cool completely.

• Combine all frosting ingredients in small bowl. Beat at medium speed until creamy. Spread over cooled bars. Drizzle with melted chocolate. Cool completely; cut into bars. Cover; store refrigerated.

Peanut Chocolate Swirl Bars

Preparation time: **20 minutes** | Baking time: **20 minutes** | 36 bars

½	cup LAND O LAKES® Butter
1¼	cups firmly packed brown sugar
2	eggs
2	teaspoons vanilla
1½	cups all-purpose flour
2	teaspoons baking powder
½	teaspoon salt
1	cup real semi-sweet chocolate chips
1	cup chopped salted peanuts

• Heat oven to 350°F. Melt butter in 3-quart saucepan over medium heat (3 to 5 minutes). Remove from heat. Stir in brown sugar, eggs and vanilla. Add flour, baking powder and salt; mix well. Gently stir in chocolate chips and peanuts.

• Spread mixture into ungreased 13×9-inch baking pan. Bake for 20 to 25 minutes or until center is firm to the touch. (DO NOT OVERBAKE.) Cool completely. Cut into bars.

Cappuccino Brownies

Preparation time: **20 minutes** | Baking time: **33 minutes** | 25 brownies

Brownie

- 1 tablespoon instant espresso powder*
- 2 teaspoons hot water
- 1 cup real semi-sweet chocolate chips
- ½ cup LAND O LAKES® Butter
- 1 cup sugar
- 1 teaspoon vanilla
- 2 eggs
- 1 cup all-purpose flour
- ½ teaspoon baking powder
- ¼ teaspoon salt

Frosting

- 1 teaspoon instant espresso powder*
- 2 to 3 tablespoons milk or cream
- 2 cups powdered sugar
- ¼ cup LAND O LAKES® Butter, softened

Drizzle

- ⅓ cup real semi-sweet chocolate chips
- ½ teaspoon shortening

• Heat oven to 350°F. Combine 1 tablespoon espresso powder and hot water in small bowl; stir to dissolve. Set aside.

• Melt 1 cup chocolate chips and ½ cup butter in 3-quart saucepan over low heat, stirring occasionally, until smooth (4 to 7 minutes). Remove from heat; stir in espresso mixture, sugar and vanilla. Add eggs, one at a time, mixing well after each addition. Add flour, baking powder and salt; stir until well mixed.

• Spread mixture into greased 8-inch square baking pan. Bake for 33 to 38 minutes or until brownies just begin to pull away from sides of pan. (DO NOT OVERBAKE.) Cool completely.

• Combine 1 teaspoon espresso powder and 2 tablespoons milk in small bowl; stir to dissolve. Add powdered sugar and ¼ cup butter. Beat at low speed, scraping bowl often and adding enough milk for desired spreading consistency. Frost cooled brownies.

• Melt ⅓ cup chocolate chips and shortening in 1-quart saucepan over low heat, stirring occasionally, until smooth (2 to 4 minutes).

• Drizzle melted chocolate over frosting; swirl with toothpick or knife for marbled effect.

*Substitute 1 tablespoon instant coffee granules.

Lemon-Butter Bars

Preparation time: **30 minutes** | Baking time: **33 minutes** | 16 bars

Crust

- 1 cup all-purpose flour
- ½ cup LAND O LAKES® Butter, softened
- ¼ cup sugar

Filling

- ¾ cup sugar
- 2 eggs
- 3 tablespoons lemon juice
- 2 tablespoons all-purpose flour
- 1 teaspoon freshly grated lemon peel
- ¼ teaspoon baking powder

Powdered sugar

• Heat oven to 350°F. Combine all crust ingredients in small bowl. Beat at low speed, scraping bowl often, until mixture resembles coarse crumbs. Press onto bottom of ungreased 8-inch square baking pan. Bake for 15 to 20 minutes or until edges are lightly browned.

• Meanwhile, combine all filling ingredients except powdered sugar in small bowl. Beat at low speed, scraping bowl often, until well mixed. Pour filling over hot, partially baked crust. Continue baking for 18 to 20 minutes or until filling is set.

• Sprinkle with powdered sugar while still warm and again when cool. Cut into bars.

Classic Chocolate Brownies

Preparation time: **20 minutes** | Baking time: **25 minutes** | **25 brownies**

> ½ cup LAND O LAKES® Butter
>
> 2 (1-ounce) squares unsweetened baking chocolate
>
> 1 (1-ounce) square semi-sweet baking chocolate
>
> 1¼ cups sugar
>
> 1½ teaspoons vanilla
>
> 3 eggs
>
> 1¼ cups all-purpose flour
>
> ¼ teaspoon salt
>
> Powdered sugar, if desired

• Heat oven to 350°F. Grease bottom only of 8- or 9-inch square baking pan. Set aside.

• Melt butter, unsweetened chocolate and semi-sweet chocolate in 2-quart saucepan over low heat, stirring occasionally, until smooth (4 to 7 minutes). Remove from heat.

• Stir in sugar and vanilla. Add eggs, one at a time, mixing well after each addition. Stir in flour and salt; mix just until all ingredients are moistened and brownie mixture is smooth. (DO NOT OVERMIX.)

• Spread brownie mixture into prepared pan. Bake for 25 to 32 minutes or until brownies just begin to pull away from sides of pan. (DO NOT OVERBAKE.) Cool completely. Sprinkle with powdered sugar, if desired.

Browned Butter Frosted Pumpkin Bars

Preparation time: **20 minutes** | Baking time: **20 minutes** | **60 bars**

Bar

- 1½ cups all-purpose flour
- 1¼ cups sugar
- 2 teaspoons baking powder
- 2 teaspoons ground cinnamon
- 1 teaspoon baking soda
- ½ teaspoon ground ginger
- ¾ cup LAND O LAKES® Butter, melted
- 1 (15-ounce) can pumpkin
- 3 eggs
- ¾ cup chopped sweetened dried cranberries

Frosting

- ½ cup LAND O LAKES® Butter
- 4 cups powdered sugar
- 1 teaspoon vanilla
- ¼ to ⅓ cup milk

• Heat oven to 350°F. Combine flour, sugar, baking powder, cinnamon, baking soda and ginger in large bowl. Stir in ¾ cup butter, pumpkin and eggs; mix well. Stir in cranberries.

• Spread batter into ungreased 15×10×1-inch jelly-roll pan. Bake for 20 to 25 minutes or until toothpick inserted in center comes out clean. Cool completely.

• Meanwhile, melt ½ cup butter in 1-quart saucepan over medium heat, stirring constantly and watching closely, until butter just starts to turn golden brown (3 to 5 minutes). (Butter will get foamy and bubble.) Immediately remove from heat. Pour into medium bowl; cool 5 minutes.

• Add powdered sugar and vanilla to cooled browned butter; mix well. Stir in enough milk for desired frosting consistency. Spread frosting over cooled bars. Cut into bars.

Raspberry Cream Cheese Bars

Preparation time: **20 minutes** | Baking time: **32 minutes** | **32 bars**

Crust

½ cup LAND O LAKES® Butter, softened

⅓ cup sugar

1½ cups all-purpose flour

Topping

3 (8-ounce) packages cream cheese, softened

¾ cup sugar

2 tablespoons cornstarch

3 eggs

¾ teaspoon almond extract

1 cup fresh or frozen red raspberries

¼ cup sliced almonds

• Heat oven to 350°F. Combine butter and ⅓ cup sugar in large bowl. Beat at medium speed, scraping bowl often, until creamy. Reduce speed to low; add flour. Beat until well mixed.

• Press mixture onto bottom of ungreased 13×9-inch baking pan. Bake for 12 to 16 minutes or until edges are very lightly browned.

• Meanwhile, combine cream cheese, ¾ cup sugar and cornstarch in large bowl. Beat at medium speed, scraping bowl often, until creamy. Add eggs and almond extract; continue beating until well mixed.

• Sprinkle raspberries over hot, partially baked crust. Pour cream cheese mixture over berries; sprinkle with almonds. Bake for 20 to 25 minutes or until set and edges are lightly browned. Run knife around outside edge of bars. Cool completely (at least 1 hour). Refrigerate bars at least 2 hours before cutting. Store refrigerated.

tip:
If using frozen raspberries, completely thaw and drain on paper towels before using.

Big Batch Fudgy Brownies

Preparation time: **15 minutes** | Baking time: **20 minutes** | 48 brownies

Brownie

- 1 cup LAND O LAKES® Butter
- 4 (1-ounce) squares unsweetened baking chocolate
- 2 cups sugar
- ½ cup LAND O LAKES® Sour Cream
- 4 eggs, slightly beaten
- 2 teaspoons vanilla
- 1¾ cups all-purpose flour
- ½ teaspoon salt

Frosting

- 1 (6-ounce) package (1 cup) real semi-sweet chocolate chips
- 2 tablespoons shortening
- 1½ cups powdered sugar
- ½ teaspoon vanilla
- 3 to 5 tablespoons milk

• Heat oven to 350°F. Melt butter and chocolate in 3-quart saucepan over low heat, stirring occasionally, until smooth (5 to 8 minutes). Remove from heat; stir in sugar. Add sour cream, eggs and 2 teaspoons vanilla; mix well. Stir in flour and salt just until moistened.

• Spread batter into greased 15×10×1-inch jelly-roll pan. Bake for 20 to 25 minutes or until brownie begins to pull away from sides of pan. (DO NOT OVERBAKE.) Cool completely.

• Melt chocolate chips and shortening in 1-quart saucepan over low heat, stirring occasionally, until smooth (3 to 5 minutes). Stir in powdered sugar, ½ teaspoon vanilla and enough milk for desired spreading consistency. Spread over cooled brownies. Cut into bars.

Southern Belle Bars

Preparation time: **10 minutes** | Baking time: **38 minutes** | **25 bars**

Crust

1¼ cups all-purpose flour

½ cup LAND O LAKES® Butter, softened

¼ cup sugar

¼ cup coarsely chopped pecans

Filling

¾ cup dark corn syrup

⅓ cup firmly packed brown sugar

2 eggs

3 tablespoons all-purpose flour

1 teaspoon vanilla

½ teaspoon salt

¾ cup coarsely chopped pecans

• Heat oven to 350°F. Combine 1¼ cups flour, butter and sugar in large bowl. Beat at medium speed, scraping bowl often, until mixture resembles coarse crumbs. Stir in ¼ cup pecans.

• Press crust mixture evenly onto bottom of ungreased 8- or 9-inch square baking pan. Bake for 18 to 22 minutes or until very light golden brown on edges.

• Meanwhile, combine all filling ingredients except pecans in small bowl; mix well. Stir in pecans. Spread evenly over hot, partially baked crust. Bake for 20 to 30 minutes or until filling appears set and knife inserted 1-inch from edge comes out clean. Cool completely; cut into bars.

Chocolate Drizzled Cherry Bars

Preparation time: **30 minutes** | Baking time: **42 minutes** | **36 bars**

Crumb Mixture

- 2 cups all-purpose flour
- 2 cups uncooked quick-cooking oats
- 1½ cups sugar
- 1¼ cups LAND O LAKES® Butter, softened

Filling

- 1 (21-ounce) can cherry pie filling
- 1 teaspoon almond extract

Drizzle

- ½ cup real semi-sweet chocolate chips
- 1 tablespoon shortening

• Heat oven to 350°F. Combine all crumb mixture ingredients in large bowl. Beat at low speed until mixture resembles coarse crumbs. Reserve 1½ cups crumb mixture; press remaining crumb mixture onto bottom of ungreased 13×9-inch baking pan. Bake for 15 to 20 minutes or until edges are very lightly browned.

• Meanwhile, combine all filling ingredients in same bowl. Spread filling over hot, partially baked crust; sprinkle with reserved crumb mixture. Continue baking for 27 to 32 minutes or until lightly browned.

• Melt chocolate chips and shortening in 1-quart saucepan over low heat, stirring constantly, until smooth (2 to 3 minutes). Drizzle over bars. Cool completely; cut into rectangles, diamonds or squares.

Berry Delicious Brownies

Preparation time: **30 minutes** | Baking time: **23 minutes** | **9 servings**

Brownie

1¼ cups sugar

¾ cup LAND O LAKES® Butter

3 (1-ounce) squares unsweetened baking chocolate

1 cup all-purpose flour

3 eggs

½ cup chopped walnuts or pecans, if desired

Topping

⅔ cup hot fudge ice cream topping, warmed

LAND O LAKES™ Heavy Whipping Cream, whipped, sweetened, if desired

Strawberries

2½ cups sliced strawberries*

1 tablespoon sugar

• Heat oven to 350°F. Grease bottom only of 8-inch square baking pan. Combine 1¼ cups sugar, butter and chocolate in 2-quart saucepan. Cook over medium heat, stirring constantly, until butter and chocolate are melted (5 to 7 minutes).

• Stir in flour and eggs until well mixed; stir in walnuts. Pour batter into prepared pan. Bake for 23 to 28 minutes or until brownies just begin to pull away from sides of pan. Cool completely. Cut into squares.

• Meanwhile, combine strawberries and 1 tablespoon sugar in small bowl.

• To serve, place brownies onto individual serving plates. Top each with 1 tablespoon warm fudge sauce and about ¼ cup strawberries. Dollop with sweetened whipped cream, if desired.

*Substitute your favorite berries.

Latte Cheesecake Bars *(photo on page 43)*

Preparation time: **20 minutes** | Baking time: **20 minutes** | **36 bars**

Crust

2 cups chocolate cookie crumbs

½ cup LAND O LAKES® Butter, melted

½ teaspoon ground cinnamon

Filling

2 tablespoons LAND O LAKES™ Heavy Whipping Cream

2 teaspoons instant coffee granules

2 (8-ounce) packages cream cheese, softened

½ cup sugar

3 eggs

½ teaspoon vanilla

Topping

⅓ cup LAND O LAKES™ Heavy Whipping Cream

½ cup real semi-sweet chocolate chips

• Heat oven to 350°F. Combine all crust ingredients in small bowl. Press onto bottom of ungreased 13×9-inch baking pan.

• Combine 2 tablespoons whipping cream and coffee granules in small bowl. Let stand 5 minutes or until coffee dissolves.

• Combine cream cheese and sugar in large bowl. Beat at medium speed, scraping bowl often, until creamy. Add coffee mixture, eggs and vanilla. Beat, scraping bowl often, just until combined. Pour over crust. Bake for 20 to 25 minutes or until center is nearly set. Cool on wire rack 1 hour.

• Place ⅓ cup whipping cream in 1-quart saucepan. Cook over medium heat until whipping cream almost comes to a boil (1 minute). Remove from heat. Stir in chocolate chips until melted. Spread over cheesecake. Refrigerate until chocolate sets, about 1 hour. Cut into bars.

Salted Nut Bars

Preparation time: **15 minutes** | Baking time: **20 minutes** | 36 bars

Crust

1½ cups all-purpose flour

¾ cup firmly packed brown sugar

½ cup LAND O LAKES® Butter, softened

¼ teaspoon salt

Topping

¼ cup light corn syrup

1 cup butterscotch-flavored baking chips

2 tablespoons LAND O LAKES® Butter

1 tablespoon water

¼ teaspoon salt

1 (11.5-ounce) can (1½ cups) mixed nuts

• Heat oven to 350°F. Spray 13×9-inch baking pan with no-stick cooking spray; set aside.

• Combine all crust ingredients in large bowl. Beat at low speed, scraping bowl often, until mixture resembles coarse crumbs. Press crumb mixture into prepared pan. Bake for 10 minutes.

• Meanwhile, place all topping ingredients except mixed nuts in 2-quart saucepan. Cook over low heat, stirring constantly, until chips are melted and mixture is smooth (5 to 7 minutes). Stir in nuts until well coated.

• Spread nut mixture over hot, partially baked crust. Continue baking for 10 to 12 minutes or until golden brown. Cool completely. Cut into bars.

Gooey Chocolate Cashew Bars

Preparation time: **15 minutes** | Baking time: **43 minutes** | **36 bars**

Crust

1½ cups all-purpose flour

½ cup LAND O LAKES® Butter, softened

¼ cup firmly packed brown sugar

Topping

¾ cup sugar

¾ cup dark corn syrup

3 eggs, slightly beaten

3 tablespoons LAND O LAKES® Butter, melted

2 teaspoons vanilla

1½ cups salted cashews, coarsely chopped

1½ cups real semi-sweet chocolate chips

• Heat oven to 350°F. Combine all crust ingredients in small bowl. Beat at low speed, scraping bowl often, until mixture resembles coarse crumbs.

• Press crumb mixture onto bottom of ungreased 13×9-inch baking pan. Bake for 15 minutes or until edges are lightly browned.

• Meanwhile, combine sugar, corn syrup, eggs, 3 tablespoons melted butter and vanilla in large bowl. Stir in cashews and chocolate chips.

• Spread topping over hot, partially baked crust. Continue baking for 28 to 33 minutes or until set. Cool completely. Cut into bars. Cover; store refrigerated.

tip:

If using a dark pan, adjust crust baking time to 12 minutes and filling baking time to 25 minutes.

Mocha Chocolate
Cheesecake, p. 64

Blueberry Cardamom Spice Cake,
(opposite page), p. 73

CAKES &
CHEESECAKES

What celebration is complete without a cake? Look inside for everything from light, lemony cupcakes perfect for high tea to decadent chocolate cakes with molten centers sure to impress all your guests.

Mocha Chocolate Cheesecake *(photo on page 62)*

Preparation time: **30 minutes** | Baking time: **50 minutes** | **12 servings**

Crust

- 1⅓ cups graham cracker crumbs
- ¼ cup LAND O LAKES® Butter, melted
- 2 tablespoons sugar

Filling

- 1 cup sugar
- ½ cup LAND O LAKES® Sour Cream
- 3 (8-ounce) packages cream cheese, softened
- 3 tablespoons all-purpose flour
- 3 eggs
- 1 tablespoon vanilla
- 2 teaspoons instant coffee granules
- 1 tablespoon hot water
- ¼ cup unsweetened cocoa
- 3 tablespoons LAND O LAKES® Butter, melted

Garnish

- 1 (1.4-ounce) English toffee bar, chopped

• Heat oven to 325°F. Stir together all crust ingredients in medium bowl. Press crumb mixture evenly onto bottom of ungreased 9-inch springform pan. Bake for 10 minutes or until golden brown. Cool completely.

• Meanwhile, combine ¾ cup sugar, sour cream, cream cheese and flour in large bowl. Beat at low speed, scraping bowl often, until creamy. Add eggs and vanilla; continue beating until well mixed. Reserve 1½ cups cream cheese mixture. Set aside.

• Combine coffee granules and water in small bowl; stir until granules dissolve. Combine remaining ¼ cup sugar, cocoa and 3 tablespoons melted butter in small bowl; stir until smooth. Add coffee and cocoa mixtures to remaining cream cheese mixture; continue beating until well mixed. Pour cocoa-cream cheese mixture into baked crust. Spoon reserved cream cheese mixture over chocolate mixture; pull knife through batter for marbled effect.

• Bake for 50 to 60 minutes or until set 2 inches from edge of pan. (Center will still be soft.) Remove from oven; let stand 10 minutes. Loosen sides of cheesecake from pan by carefully running knife around inside of pan. (Dip knife in hot water if cheesecake sticks to knife.) Do not remove sides. Cool 1 hour. Cover; refrigerate at least 4 hours. Remove sides of pan.

• To serve, garnish with chopped English toffee bar. Store refrigerated.

tip:
Using a dark nonstick springform pan may result in surface cracking.

Saucy-Center Mocha Cakes

Preparation time: **15 minutes** | Baking time: **9 minutes** | 6 servings

Cake

- 6 tablespoons LAND O LAKES® Butter
- 1 cup real semi-sweet chocolate chips
- 2 teaspoons instant coffee granules
- 3 eggs
- ½ cup sugar
- 2 tablespoons all-purpose flour
- ½ teaspoon vanilla

Topping

Powdered sugar

LAND O LAKES™ Heavy Whipping Cream, whipped, if desired

• Heat oven to 400°F. Grease and lightly flour 6 (5- or 6-ounce) glass custard cups. Place onto ungreased baking sheet. Set aside.

• Melt butter, chocolate chips and coffee granules in 1-quart saucepan over medium heat, stirring occasionally, until smooth (2 to 3 minutes). Set aside.

• Beat eggs in small bowl at high speed until slightly thickened and lemon-colored. Continue beating, gradually adding sugar, until light and fluffy. Add melted chocolate, flour and vanilla. Reduce speed to low; beat just until mixed.

• Divide batter evenly among prepared cups. Bake for 9 to 13 minutes or until top is puffy and crackled in appearance, but center is still soft. Cool 5 minutes; loosen sides of cakes by running knife around inside of cups.

• Invert cakes onto individual serving plates. Sprinkle with powdered sugar. Serve warm with whipped cream, if desired.

tip:
Batter can be prepared several hours ahead. Cover and refrigerate if more than 1 hour. Allow to stand at room temperature at least 15 minutes to warm slightly before baking. Bake just before serving.

tip:
To easily sift powdered sugar, place sugar in small strainer. Gently tap strainer to allow the sugar to fall through openings onto cakes.

tip:
Dessert can also be served with ice cream.

Root Beer Cupcakes

Preparation time: **40 minutes** | Baking time: **23 minutes** | **2 dozen cupcakes**

Cupcake

- 1 to 1¼ cups root beer
- ½ cup LAND O LAKES® Butter, softened
- 1 (18.25-ounce) package butter recipe yellow cake mix with pudding
- 3 eggs
- ⅓ cup crushed root beer-flavored candies

Frosting

- 3 cups powdered sugar
- ¼ cup LAND O LAKES® Butter, softened
- 3 to 4 tablespoons milk

  Crushed root beer-flavored candies, if desired

• Heat oven to 350°F. Use the amount of root beer (1 to 1¼ cups) as indicted for water on cake mix package.

• Combine root beer, ½ cup butter, cake mix and eggs in large bowl. Beat at low speed until moistened. Increase speed to medium. Beat until well mixed. Stir in crushed candies by hand.

• Spoon ¼ cup batter into each paper-lined muffin cup. Bake for 23 to 25 minutes or until toothpick inserted in center comes out clean. Cool 2 to 3 minutes; remove from pan. Cool completely.

• Meanwhile, combine powdered sugar and ¼ cup butter in small bowl. Beat at low speed, scraping bowl often and gradually adding enough milk for desired spreading consistency. Frost cooled cupcakes. Garnish with additional crushed root beer-flavored candies, if desired.

tip:

Be sure to use the specific weight cake mix as directed above to ensure success of this recipe.

tip:

To crush candies, place in heavy resealable plastic food bag. Crush with hammer or rolling pin on cutting board. Candies can also be crushed in small food processor or blender.

Peanut Butter Chocolate Chip Cheesecake

Preparation time: **25 minutes** | Baking time: **1 hour 10 minutes** | **12 servings**

Crust

1½ cups (15 cookies) chocolate sandwich cookie crumbs

3 tablespoons LAND O LAKES® Butter, melted

Filling

½ cup LAND O LAKES® Sour Cream

3 (8-ounce) packages cream cheese, softened

3 eggs

1 cup sugar

¾ cup creamy peanut butter

1 tablespoon cornstarch

1 cup real semi-sweet chocolate chips

• Heat oven to 325°F. Combine all crust ingredients in small bowl. Press crumb mixture evenly onto bottom of ungreased 9-inch springform pan. Bake for 10 minutes. Cool completely.

• Meanwhile, combine sour cream and cream cheese in large bowl. Beat at low speed 1 minute. Add eggs, one at a time, beating well after each addition. Add sugar, peanut butter and cornstarch. Continue beating until well mixed (1 to 2 minutes). (DO NOT OVERBEAT.) Stir in chocolate chips by hand.

• Spoon filling over cooled crust. Bake for 60 to 80 minutes or until center is almost set. (Cheesecake surface may be slightly cracked and lightly browned.)

• Immediately run knife around inside of pan to loosen sides of cheesecake. Cool 1 hour. Cover; refrigerate until completely cooled (4 hours or overnight). Remove sides of pan. Store covered in refrigerator up to 3 days.

tip:

Substitute graham crackers, gingersnaps or vanilla wafers in the crust. It is easy to crush the crackers or cookies in a food processor, or in a heavy resealable plastic food bag. Simply crush them with a rolling pin. Just make sure there are no large pieces or the crust may crumble when cut.

tip:

Most cheesecakes will puff up slightly as they bake. When baked sufficiently, the top should no longer be shiny. When you tap the side of the pan, the cheesecake will move, but not jiggle. The center will appear softer than the edges and may sink during cooling.

tip:

To freeze, follow directions above for cooling. Wrap cheesecake in plastic food wrap, then in heavy-duty aluminum foil. Label; freeze up to 2 months.

Pineapple-Filled Jelly Roll

Preparation time: **45 minutes** | Baking time: **10 minutes** | **10 servings**

Filling

- ½ cup firmly packed brown sugar
- ¼ cup LAND O LAKES® Butter
- 1 (20-ounce) can crushed pineapple in syrup, drained, reserve syrup
- ½ cup reserved pineapple syrup
- 1 tablespoon cornstarch

Cake

- Powdered sugar
- 4 eggs, separated
- ¾ cup sugar
- 1 teaspoon baking powder
- ½ teaspoon vanilla
- ¼ teaspoon salt
- ½ cup all-purpose flour

Powdered sugar, if desired
Maraschino cherries, if desired

- Combine all filling ingredients in 2-quart saucepan. Cook over medium heat, stirring occasionally, until mixture comes to a full boil (8 to 10 minutes). Boil 1 minute. Cover; refrigerate until completely cooled (2 to 3 hours).

- Heat oven to 375°F. Grease 15×10×1-inch jelly-roll pan. Line with parchment or waxed paper; grease paper. Set aside. Arrange clean towel on counter; sprinkle generously with powdered sugar. Set aside.

- Beat egg whites in small bowl at high speed until foamy. Gradually add ¼ cup sugar, beating until glossy and stiff peaks form (2 to 3 minutes). Set aside.

- Combine remaining ½ cup sugar, egg yolks, baking powder, vanilla and salt in large bowl. Beat at medium speed, scraping bowl often, until well mixed. Gently fold in egg whites, alternately with flour, until just mixed.

- Spread batter evenly into prepared pan. Bake for 10 to 15 minutes or until center springs back when lightly touched. Immediately loosen cake from edges of pan. Invert onto prepared towel. Remove pan; peel off parchment paper. While hot, starting with 10-inch side, roll up cake in towel. Cool completely.

- Unroll cooled cake; remove towel. Spread cake with cooled filling. Starting with 10-inch side, roll up cake. Transfer to serving platter. Cover; refrigerate 2 hours before serving.

- To serve, cut jelly roll into slices. Garnish with powdered sugar and cherries, if desired. Store refrigerated.

Pear & Walnut Upside-Down Cake

Preparation time: **15 minutes** | Baking time: **35 minutes** | **8 servings**

Topping

¼ cup LAND O LAKES® Butter

½ cup firmly packed brown sugar

2 medium Bartlett or Anjou pears, thinly sliced

⅓ cup chopped walnuts

Cake

½ cup firmly packed brown sugar

⅓ cup LAND O LAKES® Butter, softened

1 cup all-purpose flour

⅓ cup milk

2 eggs

1½ teaspoons baking powder

1 teaspoon vanilla

½ teaspoon ground cinnamon

¼ teaspoon salt

Vanilla or cinnamon ice cream, if desired

• Heat oven to 350°F. Melt ¼ cup butter in oven in 9-inch metal pie pan or 9-inch round baking pan. Stir in ½ cup brown sugar. Arrange pear slices over brown sugar in spoke fashion overlapping slices in center; sprinkle with walnuts. Set aside.

• Combine ½ cup brown sugar and ⅓ cup butter in large bowl. Beat at medium speed, scraping bowl often, until creamy. Add all remaining cake ingredients; continue beating until well mixed. Gently spread batter on top of pears.

• Bake for 35 to 40 minutes or until toothpick inserted in center comes out clean. Cool 5 minutes. Run knife around inside of pie pan to loosen sides of cake. Invert cake onto serving platter. Remove pie pan. Cool completely. Serve with ice cream, if desired.

tip:

This cake, served upside-down, is even "created" upside-down! The topping is made first and put in the bottom of the pie pan. The brown sugar-butter mixture caramelizes as it bakes giving the pear and nuts a delicate candy-like coating. The cake is added next and baked until golden brown. After baking, the cake is inverted and served upside-down—or is it right-side up?

Chocolate Chip Whipped Cream Loaf

Preparation time: **20 minutes** | Baking time: **45 minutes** | **10 servings**

1½ cups all-purpose flour	2 eggs
1 cup sugar	1 teaspoon vanilla
2 teaspoons baking powder	½ cup mini real semi-sweet chocolate chips
½ teaspoon salt	
1 cup LAND O LAKES™ Heavy Whipping Cream	Fresh fruit, if desired

• Heat oven to 350°F. Grease and flour 9×5-inch loaf pan; set aside. Combine flour, sugar, baking powder and salt in medium bowl; set aside.

• Beat whipping cream in large bowl at high speed until soft peaks form. Add eggs and vanilla; continue beating just until blended. Gently stir in flour mixture and chocolate chips by hand until blended.

• Pour batter into prepared pan. Bake for 45 to 55 minutes or until toothpick inserted in center comes out clean. Run knife around edges of pan to loosen; turn out onto cooling rack. Cool completely.

• To serve, cut cake into slices; serve with fresh fruit, if desired.

variation:
Omit chocolate chips. Substitute ½ cup chopped walnuts, 1 teaspoon freshly grated lemon peel or 1 teaspoon freshly grated orange peel with flour mixture.

Blueberry Cardamom Spice Cake

Preparation time: **15 minutes** | Baking time: **45 minutes** | **12 servings**

½ cup LAND O LAKES® Butter, softened

½ cup sugar

½ cup firmly packed brown sugar

3 eggs

2 cups all-purpose flour

1 cup LAND O LAKES® Sour Cream

2 teaspoons baking powder

1 teaspoon ground cardamom

¼ teaspoon ground cinnamon

¼ teaspoon ground ginger

⅛ teaspoon salt

1½ cups fresh blueberries

Powdered sugar

Fresh blueberries, if desired

• Heat oven to 350°F. Combine butter, sugar and brown sugar in large bowl. Beat at medium speed, scraping bowl often, until creamy. Add eggs, one at a time, beating well after each addition. Add all remaining ingredients except blueberries and powdered sugar. Continue beating, scraping bowl often, until well mixed. Gently stir in 1½ cups blueberries.

• Pour batter into greased and floured 12-cup Bundt® or angel food cake (tube) pan. Bake for 45 to 55 minutes or until toothpick inserted in center comes out clean. Cool 15 minutes. Loosen edges of cake from pan using metal spatula. Invert cake onto serving platter.

• To serve, sprinkle with powdered sugar. Garnish with additional blueberries, if desired.

Crazy Toffee Snack Cake

Preparation time: **15 minutes** | Baking time: **35 minutes** | **9 servings**

Cake

- 1¼ cups all-purpose flour
- ¾ cup sugar
- 1½ teaspoons baking powder
- ½ teaspoon salt
- 1 egg
- 1 teaspoon vanilla
- ½ cup LAND O LAKES® Butter, melted
- ¾ cup milk

Topping

- ½ cup all-purpose flour
- ½ cup firmly packed brown sugar
- 2 tablespoons LAND O LAKES® Butter, softened
- ½ cup milk chocolate English toffee bits*

• Heat oven to 350°F. Combine 1¼ cups flour, sugar, baking powder and salt in ungreased 8- or 9-inch square baking pan. Set aside.

• Combine egg and vanilla in small bowl with wire whisk.

• Make two indentations in flour mixture; pour egg mixture in one and ½ cup melted butter in the other. Pour milk over all; mix well with fork until flour mixture is completely moistened.

• Combine all topping ingredients except toffee bits in small bowl. Sprinkle over batter. Bake for 35 to 40 minutes or until toothpick inserted in center comes out clean. Immediately sprinkle with toffee bits. Cool completely.

*Substitute 2 (1.4-ounce) milk chocolate English toffee bars, finely chopped.

Tea Party Lemonade Cupcakes

Preparation time: **25 minutes** Baking time: **15 minutes** | **18 cupcakes**

Cupcakes

- 2 cups all-purpose flour
- 1 teaspoon baking powder
- 1 teaspoon baking soda
- ¾ cup sugar
- ½ cup LAND O LAKES® Butter, softened
- 2 eggs
- ½ cup frozen lemonade concentrate, thawed
- ¼ cup milk

Frosting

- 6 tablespoons LAND O LAKES® Butter, softened
- 3 cups powdered sugar
- 4 to 5 tablespoons frozen lemonade concentrate, thawed

  Candy fruit slices, cut as desired

• Heat oven to 350°F. Combine flour, baking powder and baking soda in small bowl. Set aside.

• Combine sugar and ½ cup butter in large bowl. Beat at medium speed until creamy. Add eggs, ½ cup lemonade concentrate and milk; continue beating until well mixed. Reduce speed to low; add flour mixture. Beat, scraping bowl often, until well mixed.

• Spoon batter into 18 paper-lined muffin cups. Bake for 15 to 18 minutes or until toothpick inserted in center comes out clean. Cool 10 minutes; remove from pans. Cool completely.

• Meanwhile, place 6 tablespoons butter in medium bowl; beat at medium speed until creamy. Continue beating, scraping bowl often and gradually adding powdered sugar and enough lemonade concentrate for desired frosting consistency. Frost cooled cupcakes. Garnish with candy fruit slices, if desired.

Raspberry Cheesecake with Chocolate Crust

Preparation time: **40 minutes** | Baking time: **1 hour** | **16 servings**

Filling

1 (12-ounce) package frozen raspberries, partially thawed

2 tablespoons cornstarch

Crust

1 (9-ounce) package chocolate wafer cookies*

⅓ cup LAND O LAKES® Butter, melted

Cheesecake

1½ cups sugar

2 (8-ounce) packages cream cheese, softened

4 eggs

1½ cups LAND O LAKES® Sour Cream

3 tablespoons cornstarch

1 teaspoon vanilla

½ cup LAND O LAKES® Sour Cream

• Combine raspberries and 2 tablespoons cornstarch in 2-quart saucepan. Cook over medium heat, stirring constantly, until mixture comes to a boil (6 to 10 minutes). Continue boiling 1 minute. Remove from heat. Cool 10 minutes. Cover; refrigerate.

• Heat oven to 325°F. Place chocolate cookies in food processor bowl fitted with metal blade. Cover; process until very finely chopped (30 to 40 seconds). Add butter; process until smooth (20 to 30 seconds). Press onto bottom of 9-inch springform pan. Set aside.

• Combine sugar and cream cheese in large bowl. Beat at medium speed, scraping bowl often, until creamy. Add eggs, one at a time, beating well after each addition (1 to 2 minutes). Add 1½ cups sour cream and 3 tablespoons cornstarch. Continue beating, scraping bowl often, until well mixed (1 to 2 minutes). Stir in vanilla.

• Pour half of cheesecake batter over chocolate crust. Stir ½ cup sour cream into cooled filling; spoon evenly over cheesecake batter in pan. Top with remaining cheesecake batter. Bake for 60 to 70 minutes or until just set 2 inches from edge of pan. Turn off oven; leave cheesecake in oven 2 hours. Remove from oven. Loosen sides of cheesecake from pan by running knife around inside of pan. Cool completely (about 2 hours). Loosely cover; refrigerate 8 hours or overnight.

*Substitute chocolate graham crackers 32 (2½×2½-inch) squares or 16 (4¾×2½-inch) rectangles.

microwave directions for filling:

Combine raspberries and 2 tablespoons cornstarch in 2-quart microwave-safe dish. Microwave on HIGH, stirring frequently, until mixture comes to a boil (6 to 8 minutes). Continue microwaving on HIGH 1 minute. Remove from microwave. Continue as directed above.

Cappuccino Roulade

Preparation time: **30 minutes** | Baking time: **9 minutes** | **10 servings**

Cake

Powdered sugar

¾ cup all-purpose flour

¼ cup unsweetened cocoa

⅛ teaspoon salt

4 eggs

⅔ cup sugar

3 tablespoons LAND O LAKES® Butter, melted, cooled

Filling

1¼ cups LAND O LAKES™ Heavy Whipping Cream

1 teaspoon instant espresso powder

2 tablespoons powdered sugar

⅛ teaspoon ground cinnamon

Sauce

⅓ cup water

4 (1-ounce) squares semi-sweet baking chocolate, chopped

2 tablespoons LAND O LAKES® Butter

½ teaspoon instant espresso powder

⅛ teaspoon ground cinnamon

• Heat oven to 375°F. Grease 15×10×1-inch jelly-roll pan; line with parchment paper. Grease and flour parchment paper; set aside.

• Lightly sprinkle clean towel with powdered sugar; set aside. Combine flour, ¼ cup cocoa and salt in medium bowl; set aside.

• Beat eggs in large bowl at medium-high speed until well mixed. Continue beating, gradually adding sugar, until mixture is thick and lemon-colored. Gently stir flour mixture into egg mixture, one-third at a time, stirring just until combined after each addition. Remove 1 cup batter; gently stir together with 3 tablespoons melted butter in small bowl. Working quickly, gently stir butter mixture into batter.

• Spread batter into prepared pan. Bake for 9 to 12 minutes or until center springs back lightly when touched. Immediately loosen cake from edges of pan. Invert onto prepared towel. Remove pan; peel off parchment paper. Immediately roll up cake in towel, starting with 10-inch side. Cool completely. (Trim edges slightly, if crisp.)

• Stir together whipping cream and 1 teaspoon espresso powder in large bowl until espresso powder is dissolved. Beat at medium speed until stiff peaks form. Gently stir in powdered sugar and ⅛ teaspoon cinnamon.

• Unroll cooled cake; remove towel. Spread whipped cream over surface of cake, leaving a ½-inch border all around. Starting at short end, gently roll up cake. Transfer to serving platter. Cover; refrigerate until ready to serve.

• Combine all sauce ingredients in 1-quart saucepan. Cook over low heat, stirring constantly, until chocolate is melted (2 to 4 minutes).

• To serve, cut roulade into slices. Spoon sauce onto each dessert plate; top with roulade slice.

Double Chocolate Almond Cake

Preparation time: **15 minutes** | Baking time: **55 minutes** | **16 servings**

Cake

- 1 cup LAND O LAKES® Sour Cream
- ½ cup chocolate-flavored syrup
- ¼ cup water
- 1 (19.8 to 21.5-ounce) box plain brownie mix
- ½ (18.25-ounce) box (2 cups) devil's food cake mix
- 3 eggs
- 2 teaspoons almond extract
- 2 teaspoons vanilla
- ¾ cup chopped almonds, toasted

Chocolate glaze

- 1 cup real semi-sweet chocolate chips
- 3 tablespoons LAND O LAKES® Butter
- 2 tablespoons LAND O LAKES™ Half & Half
- 1 tablespoon vegetable oil
- 1 teaspoon almond extract

  Fresh currants, if desired

- Heat oven to 350°F. Generously spray 12-cup Bundt® pan with no-stick cooking spray; set aside.

- Combine all cake ingredients except almonds in large bowl. Beat at low speed, scraping bowl often, until well mixed. Stir in toasted almonds by hand.

- Pour batter into prepared pan. Bake for 55 to 65 minutes or until cake begins to pull away from sides of pan. (DO NOT OVERBAKE.) Cool 10 minutes; invert onto serving plate. Cool completely.

- Meanwhile, combine all chocolate glaze ingredients except almond extract in 1-quart saucepan. Cook over low heat, stirring constantly, until chips are melted and mixture is smooth (2 to 3 minutes). Stir in 1 teaspoon almond extract. Drizzle over cooled cake. Garnish with fresh currants, if desired.

tip:

Make cupcakes with remaining cake mix. In small bowl, combine remaining half box of cake mix, ¾ cup water, 2 tablespoons vegetable oil and 2 eggs. Beat at medium speed for 2 minutes. Spoon batter into paper-lined muffin cups filling each about two-thirds full. Bake at 350°F. for 19 to 23 minutes or until toothpick inserted in center comes out clean. Cool completely. Sprinkle each with powdered sugar or top with your favorite frosting. Makes 12 cupcakes.

Chocolate Mint Pinwheels, p. 94

Chocolate Caramel Shortbread Fingers
(opposite page), p. 87

COOKIES

Everyone has a favorite cookie—some people crave chocolate treats, some go crazy for nuts and still others are fans of fruit flavors. Whatever your preferences may be, you're sure to find several new favorites in this amazing collection of cookie recipes.

Soft Sugar Cookies

Preparation time: **30 minutes** | Baking time: **6 minutes per pan** | 3 dozen cookies

1½ cups sugar

1 cup LAND O LAKES® Butter, softened

2 eggs

2 teaspoons freshly grated orange peel

1 teaspoon vanilla

4⅓ cups all-purpose flour

1 teaspoon baking powder

1 teaspoon baking soda

½ teaspoon salt

1 cup LAND O LAKES® Sour Cream

Decorator sugars

• Combine sugar, butter, eggs, orange peel and vanilla in large bowl. Beat at medium speed, scraping bowl often, until creamy. Reduce speed to low; add flour, baking powder, baking soda and salt alternately with sour cream until well mixed.

• Divide dough into thirds; wrap each in plastic food wrap. Refrigerate until firm (at least 2 hours).

• Heat oven to 400°F. Roll out dough on lightly floured surface, one-third at a time (keeping remaining dough refrigerated), to ¼-inch thickness. Cut with 3-inch cookie cutters. Place 1 inch apart onto ungreased cookie sheets. Sprinkle with decorator sugars, as desired. Bake for 6 to 9 minutes or until edges are lightly browned.

Sparkling Butter Toffee Cookies

Preparation time: **30 minutes** | Baking time: **9 minutes per pan** | **5 dozen cookies**

1 cup sugar

¾ cup LAND O LAKES® Butter, softened

1 egg

1 teaspoon vanilla

2 cups all-purpose flour

1½ teaspoons baking powder

¼ teaspoon baking soda

½ cup English or almond toffee bits

Sugar

• Heat oven to 350°F. Combine sugar, butter, egg and vanilla in large bowl. Beat at medium speed, scraping bowl often, until creamy. Reduce speed to low; add flour, baking powder and baking soda. Beat until well mixed. Stir in toffee bits by hand.

• Shape dough into 1-inch balls. Roll in sugar. Place 2 inches apart onto ungreased cookie sheets. Flatten each ball with bottom of glass to 1½-inch circle. (If glass sticks, dip glass in sugar.)

• Bake for 9 to 11 minutes or until edges are just lightly browned. (DO NOT OVERBAKE.) Sprinkle with sugar while warm. Cool completely.

tip:
English toffee bits are available in the baking section of large supermarkets.

tip:
Cookies may also be flattened with a fork in a crisscross pattern.

English Lemon Shortbread Strips

Preparation time: **15 minutes** | Baking time: **35 minutes** | **2½ dozen cookies**

Shortbread

- 1 cup LAND O LAKES® Butter, softened
- ½ cup sugar
- 2 tablespoons lemon juice
- 2 teaspoons finely grated lemon peel
- 2¼ cups all-purpose flour

Glaze

- ½ cup powdered sugar
- 1 tablespoon LAND O LAKES® Butter, softened
- 1 tablespoon lemon juice

Garnish

- 1 tablespoon finely grated lemon peel

• Heat oven to 350°F. Combine all shortbread ingredients except flour in large bowl. Beat at medium speed, scraping bowl often, until creamy. Reduce speed to low; add flour. Beat until mixture resembles coarse crumbs.

• Press dough evenly into lightly greased 8-inch square baking pan. Bake for 35 to 40 minutes or until light golden brown. Cool completely.

• Combine powdered sugar, 1 tablespoon butter and 1 tablespoon lemon juice in small bowl using wire whisk; mix until smooth.

• Spread thin layer of glaze over cooled shortbread; sprinkle with 1 tablespoon lemon peel. Let stand 30 minutes to set. Cut into strips.

Chocolate Caramel Shortbread Fingers

Preparation time: **20 minutes** | Baking time: **22 minutes** | **30 cookies**

Cookie

- ½ cup LAND O LAKES® Butter, softened
- ¼ cup powdered sugar
- 2 tablespoons firmly packed brown sugar
- 1¼ cups all-purpose flour
- ¾ teaspoon baking powder
- ¼ teaspoon salt

Topping

- ⅓ cup caramel ice cream topping
- ¼ cup slivered almonds, coarsely chopped
- 2 ounces milk chocolate, chopped

- Heat oven to 325°F. Line 8-inch square baking pan with aluminum foil leaving a 1-inch overhang.

- Combine butter, powdered sugar and brown sugar in large bowl. Beat at medium speed, scraping bowl often, until creamy. Reduce speed to low; add flour, baking powder and salt. Beat until well mixed.

- Press dough into prepared pan; prick with fork every ½ inch. Bake for 22 to 25 minutes or until lightly browned. Lift cookies from pan using aluminum foil. Place on cutting board. Immediately cut into 30 (2¾×¾-inch) pieces.

- Place caramel topping in small saucepan. Cook over medium heat, stirring constantly, until caramel has slightly thickened (2 to 3 minutes). Remove from heat; drizzle caramel over cookies. Sprinkle with almonds. Cool to lukewarm; carefully separate. Cool completely.

- Melt chocolate in small microwave-safe dish on MEDIUM (50% power) until soft (1 to 1½ minutes). Stir until smooth. Drizzle over cooled cookies. Let stand until set.

Chocolate-Dipped Citrus Ribbons

Preparation time: **45 minutes** | Baking time: **7 minutes per pan** | **6½ dozen cookies**

Cookie

- 1 cup LAND O LAKES® Butter, softened
- ⅔ cup sugar
- 1 egg
- 1 tablespoon orange juice
- 1½ teaspoons freshly grated orange peel
- ½ teaspoon vanilla
- 2½ cups all-purpose flour

Dip

- 1 cup white baking chips
- 2 tablespoons shortening
- 1 cup real semi-sweet chocolate chips

• Heat oven to 350°F. Combine all cookie ingredients except flour in large bowl. Beat at medium speed, scraping bowl often, until creamy. Reduce speed to low; add flour. Beat until well mixed.

• Fit cookie press with ribbon template. Fill cookie press with dough. Press long continuous strips of dough onto ungreased cookie sheet; score every 3 inches. Bake for 7 to 9 minutes or until edges are lightly browned. Cut or break apart on cuts. Cool completely.

• Meanwhile, melt white baking chips and 1 tablespoon shortening in 1-quart saucepan over low heat, stirring occasionally, until smooth (3 to 4 minutes). Melt chocolate chips and remaining shortening in another 1-quart saucepan over low heat, stirring occasionally, until smooth (3 to 4 minutes). Pour melted mixtures side by side into a shallow dish; swirl with knife for marbled effect. Dip one end of each cookie into marbled mixture. Place cookies on cooling rack over waxed paper to set.

variation:

Lemon or Lime Ribbons: Substitute 1½ teaspoons finely grated lemon or lime peel and 1 tablespoon lemon or lime juice for orange peel and juice.

Double Dip Chocolate Slices

Preparation time: **40 minutes** | Baking time: **10 minutes per pan** | **6½ dozen cookies**

Cookie

- 1 cup sugar
- 1 cup LAND O LAKES® Butter, softened
- 1 egg
- 1 tablespoon milk
- ½ teaspoon peppermint extract
- 3 (1-ounce) squares semi-sweet baking chocolate, melted, cooled
- 2½ cups all-purpose flour
- ¼ teaspoon baking powder
- ¼ teaspoon salt

Coating

- 20 ounces vanilla-flavored candy coating
- ½ teaspoon peppermint extract
- 4 to 8 drops green food color
- 11 (1-ounce) squares semi-sweet baking chocolate
- 1 tablespoon shortening

• Combine sugar and butter in large bowl. Beat at medium speed, scraping bowl often, until creamy. Add egg, milk and peppermint extract; continue beating until well mixed. Add 3 ounces melted chocolate; continue beating until well mixed. Reduce speed to low. Add flour, baking powder and salt; beat until well mixed.

• Divide dough in half; shape each half into 8×1¾-inch long log. Wrap each log in waxed paper or plastic food wrap. Refrigerate 2 hours or overnight.

• Heat oven to 350°F. Re-shape each dough half into a round roll before unwrapping, if necessary. Cut logs into thin ⅛-inch slices with sharp knife. (If cookies are cut too thick, they will not be crisp.) Place 1 inch apart onto ungreased cookie sheets. Bake for 10 to 12 minutes or until set. Cool 1 minute; remove from cookie sheets. Cool completely.

• Melt candy coating in 2-quart saucepan over low heat, stirring often, until smooth. Remove from heat. Stir in peppermint extract and food color. Tipping saucepan slightly, dip cookies halfway into melted coating. Lightly shake off excess coating. Place on waxed paper. Let stand until coating is firm (at least 20 minutes).

• Melt 11 ounces semi-sweet baking chocolate and 1 tablespoon shortening in 1-quart saucepan over low heat, stirring occasionally, until smooth (6 to 8 minutes). Remove from heat. Tipping saucepan slightly, dip cookies into melted chocolate, overlapping half of green coating. Lightly shake off excess coating. Place on waxed paper at least 2 hours or refrigerate 20 minutes to set chocolate. Store in single layer between sheets of waxed paper in loosely covered container in cool place.

tip:

Vanilla candy coating is sometimes called almond bark coating. It is sold in the baking or candy aisle of your supermarket. It is usually packaged in trays of cubes in 16-ounce or 20-ounce packages.

tip:

If coating or chocolate becomes too thick, reheat over low heat until melted.

tip:

If dough is chilled for more than 2 hours, allow to stand at room temperature 10 to 20 minutes before slicing.

Cocoa Macadamia Nut Sandies

Preparation time: **35 minutes** | Baking time: **18 minutes per pan** | **5 dozen cookies**

- 1 cup LAND O LAKES® Butter, softened
- ½ cup sugar
- ¼ cup unsweetened cocoa
- 1 tablespoon water
- 2 teaspoons vanilla
- 2 cups all-purpose flour
- 1 (3.25 ounce) jar (⅔ cup) macadamia nuts, finely chopped
- ¾ cup powdered sugar

• Heat oven to 325°F. Combine butter and sugar in large bowl. Beat at medium speed, scraping bowl often, until well mixed. Add cocoa, water and vanilla; continue beating until well mixed. Reduce speed to low; add flour. Beat until well mixed. Stir in macadamia nuts by hand.

• Shape dough into 1-inch balls. Place 1 inch apart onto ungreased cookie sheets. Bake for 18 to 20 minutes or until set. Remove from cookie sheets. Cool completely. Roll in powdered sugar.

tip:
Want a little variety? Substitute finely chopped blanched hazelnuts or walnuts for the macadamia nuts. Still need more options? Add ¼ teaspoon almond extract or coconut flavoring along with the vanilla.

Orange Cardamom Shortbread Wedges

Preparation time: **20 minutes** | Baking time: **20 minutes** | **32 shortbread wedges**

Shortbread

- 1 cup LAND O LAKES® Butter, very soft
- ½ cup sugar
- 2 teaspoons freshly grated orange peel
- 1 teaspoon vanilla
- 2½ cups all-purpose flour
- 1 teaspoon ground cardamom*

Glaze

- ½ cup orange marmalade, melted

• Heat oven to 350°F. Combine butter, sugar, orange peel and vanilla in large bowl. Beat at medium speed, scraping bowl often, until creamy. Reduce speed to low; add flour and cardamom. Beat until mixture resembles coarse crumbs.

• Press mixture evenly into two ungreased (9-inch) round baking pans. Bake for 20 to 25 minutes or until edges are light golden brown. Cool 10 minutes. Immediately cut each pan into 16 wedges. Cool in pans 1 hour.

• Lightly brush shortbread with melted orange marmalade. Remove from pans.

*Substitute 1 teaspoon ground cinnamon.

tip:

Spread orange marmalade with a pastry brush to evenly distribute the orange rind.

Chocolate Mint Pinwheels

Preparation time: **40 minutes** | Baking time: **7 minutes per pan** | **4 dozen cookies**

½ cup sugar

½ cup LAND O LAKES® Butter, softened

1 egg

1 teaspoon vanilla

¼ teaspoon peppermint extract

1½ cups all-purpose flour

½ teaspoon baking powder

¼ teaspoon salt

1 (1-ounce) square unsweetened baking chocolate, melted, cooled

2 to 3 drops green food color

• Combine sugar, butter, egg, vanilla and peppermint extract in large bowl. Beat at medium speed, scraping bowl often, until creamy. Reduce speed to low; add flour, baking powder and salt. Beat until well mixed.

• Remove half of dough. Add cooled melted chocolate to remaining dough in bowl. Beat until well mixed. Add green food color to white dough; mix well. Shape each half into 5×4-inch rectangle; wrap in plastic food wrap. Refrigerate 1 hour.

• Roll out chocolate dough between two sheets of lightly floured waxed paper to 12×7-inch rectangle. Repeat with green dough. Place green dough on top of chocolate dough. Gently press doughs together. Roll up, jelly-roll fashion, starting with 12-inch side; wrap in plastic food wrap. Refrigerate until firm (at least 2 hours).

• Heat oven to 375°F. Cut rolls with sharp knife into ¼-inch slices. Place 1 inch apart onto ungreased cookie sheets. Bake for 7 to 9 minutes or until set. Remove from cookie sheets; cool completely.

Tiny Apricot Almond Squares

Preparation time: **20 minutes** | Baking time: **20 minutes** | 70 bars

> 1 cup sugar
>
> ½ cup LAND O LAKES® Butter, softened
>
> 1 egg
>
> ½ teaspoon almond extract
>
> 1¾ cups all-purpose flour
>
> 2 teaspoons baking powder
>
> ¼ teaspoon salt
>
> 1 cup apricot preserves
>
> ¾ cup sliced almonds
>
> Powdered sugar

• Heat oven to 350°F. Line 15×10×1-inch jelly-roll pan with aluminum foil. Lightly spray with no stick cooking spray; set aside. Combine sugar and butter in large bowl. Beat at medium speed until creamy. Add egg and almond extract; continue beating until well mixed. Reduce speed to low; add flour, baking powder and salt. Beat until well mixed.

• Pat mixture evenly into prepared pan. Spread apricot preserves evenly over batter. Sprinkle almonds evenly over preserves. Bake for 20 to 25 minutes or until set and just beginning to brown. Cool completely. Sprinkle with powdered sugar. Cut into 1½-inch squares.

variation:

Raspberry-Apricot Squares: Use ½ cup apricot preserves and ½ cup raspberry preserves. Spread apricot preserves over half of batter and raspberry preserves over other half of batter.

Maple Glazed Nut Drops

Preparation time: **30 minutes** | Baking time: **6 minutes per pan** | **10 dozen cookies**

1 cup firmly packed brown sugar

¾ cup LAND O LAKES® Butter, softened

1 egg

1½ teaspoons maple flavoring

1 teaspoon vanilla

1¾ cups all-purpose flour

Sugar

1 cup honey-roasted whole cashews*

• Heat oven to 350°F. Combine brown sugar and butter in large bowl. Beat at medium speed until creamy. Add egg, maple flavoring and vanilla; continue beating until well mixed. Reduce speed to low; add flour. Beat until well mixed.

• Shape scant teaspoonfuls of dough into ¾-inch balls; roll in sugar. Place 1 inch apart onto ungreased cookie sheets. Press 1 cashew into center of each cookie. Bake for 6 to 9 minutes or until set.

*Substitute 1 cup praline glazed nuts.

Chocolate & Orange Marbled Cookies

Preparation time: **45 minutes** | Baking time: **10 minutes per pan** | 3 dozen cookies

- ½ cup LAND O LAKES® Butter, softened
- ½ cup sugar
- ½ cup firmly packed brown sugar
- ½ cup LAND O LAKES® Sour Cream
- 1 egg
- 2 tablespoons orange juice
- 1 teaspoon freshly grated orange peel
- 1 teaspoon vanilla
- 2 cups all-purpose flour
- ½ teaspoon baking soda
- ¼ teaspoon salt
- 1 (1-ounce) square unsweetened baking chocolate, melted, cooled

• Heat oven to 350°F. Combine butter, sugar and brown sugar in large bowl. Beat at medium speed, scraping bowl often, until creamy. Add sour cream, egg, orange juice, orange peel and vanilla; continue beating until well mixed. Reduce speed to low; add flour, baking soda and salt. Beat, scraping bowl often, until well mixed.

• Pour cooled melted chocolate over batter; swirl batter with knife for marbled effect.

• Drop dough by rounded teaspoonfuls 2 inches apart onto ungreased cookie sheets. Bake for 10 to 12 minutes or until lightly browned.

Orange Cornmeal Crisps

Preparation time: **30 minutes** | Baking time: **8 minutes per pan** | **7 dozen cookies**

1 cup sugar	1 tablespoon freshly grated orange peel
1 cup LAND O LAKES® Butter, softened	2 teaspoons baking powder
1 egg	½ teaspoon ground nutmeg
2 cups all-purpose flour	
¾ cup cornmeal	Decorator sugar

• Combine 1 cup sugar, butter and egg in large bowl. Beat at medium speed, scraping bowl often, until creamy. Reduce speed to low; add all remaining ingredients except additional sugar. Beat until mixture forms a dough.

• Divide dough in half. Shape each half into 12×1½×1½-inch log. Wrap each in plastic food wrap. Refrigerate until firm (at least 1 hour).

• Heat oven to 375°F. Cut logs into ¼-inch slices with sharp knife. Place 1 inch apart onto ungreased cookie sheets. Press cookies with fork dipped in sugar to make crisscross design. Bake for 8 to 12 minutes or until edges are lightly browned.

Saucepan Molasses Cookies

Preparation time: **30 minutes** │ Baking time: **7 minutes per pan** │ **3 dozen cookies**

⅔ cup LAND O LAKES® Butter

¾ cup firmly packed brown sugar

⅓ cup light or dark molasses

1 egg

1 teaspoon vanilla

2¼ cups all-purpose flour

1 teaspoon baking soda

1 teaspoon ground cinnamon

½ teaspoon baking powder

½ teaspoon ground ginger

• Heat oven to 375°F. Melt butter in 3-quart saucepan over low heat, stirring constantly. Stir in brown sugar and molasses. Remove from heat. Stir in egg and vanilla until well mixed. Stir in all remaining ingredients just until combined.

• Drop dough by rounded teaspoonfuls, 2 inches apart, onto ungreased cookie sheets. Bake for 7 to 9 minutes or until set.

Strawberry Cheesecake Tart, p. 108

Chocolate Mint French Silk Pie
(opposite page), p. 110

DELICIOUS
PIES

There's a reason we say "as easy as pie." Perhaps no other dessert is more of an ideal treat, or so universally loved. A good pie appeals to everyone, and these pies—whether with a crisp, flaky crust or smooth, creamy filling—offer everyone a little something to dream about.

Chocolate Banana Cream Pie

Preparation time: **20 minutes** | Chilling time: **1 hour** | **8 servings**

Pie

- 2 medium bananas, sliced
- 1 (9-inch) graham cracker pie crust
- 2 cups milk
- 1 cup LAND O LAKES® Sour Cream
- 1 (3.9-ounce) package chocolate-flavor instant pudding and pie filling mix
- 1 (3.4-ounce) package banana-cream flavor instant pudding and pie filling mix
- ½ cup LAND O LAKES™ Heavy Whipping Cream, whipped

Garnish

LAND O LAKES™ Heavy Whipping Cream, whipped, if desired

Banana slices, if desired

Chocolate curls, if desired

• Arrange banana slices over bottom of pie crust. Combine all remaining pie ingredients except whipped cream in medium bowl. Beat at medium speed, scraping bowl occasionally, until mixture is smooth and thickened. Reserve ¼ cup pudding mixture.

• Pour remaining pudding mixture over bananas in pie crust. Carefully spread 1 cup whipped cream over pie. Drop reserved pudding mixture by teaspoonfuls over whipped cream. Gently swirl pudding into whipped cream using spatula or knife. Refrigerate at least 1 hour.

• At serving time, garnish pie with additional whipped cream, banana slices and chocolate curls, if desired. Store refrigerated.

Creamy Pistachio Pie

Preparation time: **15 minutes** | **8 servings**

1 (3.4-ounce) package pistachio instant pudding and pie filling mix
¾ cup milk
1 cup LAND O LAKES® Sour Cream
1 cup LAND O LAKES™ Heavy Whipping Cream, whipped, sweetened
1 (6-ounce) prepared graham cracker crumb crust

2 tablespoons shelled, pistachios, coarsely chopped

• Combine pudding mix and milk in medium bowl; stir with wire whisk until thickened. Stir in sour cream. Gently stir in 1 cup whipped cream.

• Spoon pistachio mixture into crumb crust. Spread remaining whipped cream over pistachio filling. Refrigerate until set (1 hour or overnight).

• To serve, cut pie into wedges. Sprinkle with pistachios. Store refrigerated.

Chocolate Lover's Ice Cream Pie

Preparation time: **20 minutes** | **8 servings**

24 (2 cups) crisp chocolate chip cookies, crushed
⅓ cup LAND O LAKES® Butter, melted
1 quart (4 cups) chocolate ice cream, slightly softened

Chocolate-flavored syrup
LAND O LAKES™ Heavy Whipping Cream, whipped, sweetened, if desired
Crisp chocolate chip cookies, broken into pieces, if desired

• Stir together crushed cookies and butter in medium bowl; press onto bottom and up sides of ungreased 9-inch pie pan. Freeze until firm (10 minutes).

• Spread softened ice cream over crust. Cover; freeze until firm (6 hours or overnight).

• Just before serving, drizzle pie with chocolate syrup. Garnish with sweetened whipped cream and chocolate chip cookie pieces, if desired.

Chocolate Fantasy Tarts

Preparation time: **45 minutes** | Baking time: **14 minutes** | 35 tarts

Tarts

35 (1¾×1¼-inch) mini paper liners

⅔ cup real semi-sweet chocolate chips

½ cup LAND O LAKES® Butter

¾ cup sugar

2 eggs

1 teaspoon vanilla

½ cup all-purpose flour

Fillings

see variations below

Glaze

1 cup real semi-sweet chocolate chips

3 tablespoons LAND O LAKES® Butter

2 tablespoons LAND O LAKES™ Half & Half

1 tablespoon vegetable oil

Garnishes

Sliced miniature marshmallows, maraschino cherries, mint parfait thins, round bite-sized versions of your favorite candy bar

• Heat oven to 375°F. Line mini muffin pans with paper liners or place paper liners onto baking sheets. Set aside.

• Combine ⅔ cup chocolate chips and ½ cup butter in 1-quart saucepan. Cook over low heat, stirring occasionally, until melted and smooth (5 to 7 minutes). Pour into medium bowl; cool 5 minutes.

• Stir sugar, eggs and vanilla into chocolate mixture. Gradually stir in flour until smooth. Spoon about 2 teaspoons batter into each liner, filling cups ½ full. Bake for 12 to 14 minutes or until toothpick inserted in center comes out clean.

• Remove from oven; immediately press one of the desired fillings into center of each tart.

  Marshmallow – press 3 miniature marshmallows into each tart.

  Maraschino cherry – press 1 maraschino cherry into each tart.

  Mint – break unwrapped mint parfait thins in half; press half into each tart.

  Candy bar – press 1 round bite-sized candy bar into each tart.

• Continue baking 2 minutes. Remove from pans and cool at least 5 minutes on cooling rack.

• Meanwhile, combine all glaze ingredients in 1-quart saucepan. Cook over low heat, stirring constantly, until chips are melted and mixture is smooth (2 to 3 minutes). Cool 5 minutes.

• Top each tart with about 1 teaspoon glaze. Refrigerate at least 1 hour to set glaze. Garnish if desired. Store at room temperature in container with tight fitting lid up to 3 days.

tip:
Tarts can be made ahead and frozen up to 2 months. Cool completely and store between sheets of waxed paper in container with tight-fitting lid.

tip:
Refrigerate any left over glaze and use for ice cream or dessert topping.

Strawberry Cheesecake Tart

Preparation time: **10 minutes** | Baking time: **15 minutes** | **10 servings**

Crust

- ½ cup LAND O LAKES® Butter, softened
- ⅓ cup sugar
- 1¼ cups all-purpose flour
- 2 tablespoons milk
- ½ teaspoon almond extract

Filling

- 1 cup LAND O LAKES™ Heavy Whipping Cream
- 1 (3.4-ounce) package cheesecake-flavored instant pudding, and pie filling mix
- 1 (8-ounce) package cream cheese, softened

Topping

- 1 pint fresh strawberries, hulled, sliced*
- ¼ cup strawberry jam, melted

• Heat oven to 400°F. Combine butter and sugar in small bowl. Beat at medium speed, scraping bowl often, until light and fluffy. Add flour, milk and almond extract. Reduce speed to low; beat, scraping bowl often, until mixture leaves sides of bowl and forms a ball.

• Press dough onto bottom and up sides of greased 10-inch tart pan or 12-inch pizza pan; prick with fork. Bake for 15 to 18 minutes or until light golden brown. Cool completely.

• Combine all filling ingredients in medium bowl. Beat at medium speed, scraping bowl often, until creamy. Spread over cooled crust. Refrigerate at least 1 hour.

• Just before serving, arrange strawberries over filling; brush or drizzle strawberries with melted jam.

*Substitute your favorite fruit such as blueberries or raspberries.

Butterscotch Angel Pie

Preparation time: **35 minutes** | Baking time: **1 hour** | **8 servings**

Meringue Shell

- 3 large egg whites, at room temperature
- 1 teaspoon vanilla
- ¼ teaspoon cream of tartar
- ¾ cup sugar

Filling

- 1¾ cups LAND O LAKES™ Fat Free Half & Half
- 1 egg
- 1 egg yolk
- 3 tablespoons cornstarch
- ¼ cup LAND O LAKES® Butter
- 1 cup firmly packed dark brown sugar
- 1½ teaspoons vanilla

Garnish

- 1½ cups LAND O LAKES™ Heavy Whipping Cream
- 2 tablespoons sugar
- 1 teaspoon vanilla
- 1½ cups fresh raspberries

- Heat oven to 275°F. Lightly grease and flour 9½-inch (deep-dish) pie pan. Beat egg whites, vanilla and cream of tartar in medium bowl at low speed until frothy. Increase speed to high; gradually add ¾ cup sugar, beating until stiff peaks form and mixture is glossy (2 to 3 minutes). Spread onto bottom and up sides of pie pan with back of spoon.

- Bake for 1 hour without opening oven door. Turn off oven; let meringue shell stand in oven for 1 additional hour. Remove from oven; cool to room temperature.

- Meanwhile, place ½ cup half & half, egg and egg yolk in small bowl; mix well. Stir in cornstarch with wire whisk until dissolved.

- Combine butter and brown sugar in 2-quart saucepan. Cook over low heat, stirring occasionally, until butter is melted and mixture bubbles (3 to 4 minutes).

- Stir remaining 1¼ cups half & half into butter mixture, whisking until smooth. Increase heat to medium-high; stir in cornstarch mixture. Cook, stirring occasionally, until mixture is thickened (4 to 5 minutes). Remove from heat; stir in vanilla. Place plastic food wrap directly on surface of filling. Cool 30 minutes.

- Spread filling into meringue shell. Cover; refrigerate at least 12 hours or overnight. Before serving, beat whipping cream in small bowl at high speed until soft peaks form. Add 2 tablespoons sugar and 1 teaspoon vanilla; continue beating until stiff peaks form. Spread over filling; top with raspberries.

tip:

This is an excellent "do ahead" dessert. By refrigerating the filled meringue shell, the moisture from the filling combines with the meringue to create a creamy, luscious pie.

Chocolate Mint French Silk Pie

Preparation time: **30 minutes** | Baking time: **8 minutes** | **10 servings**

Crust

- 1 cup all-purpose flour
- ⅛ teaspoon salt
- 6 tablespoons cold LAND O LAKES® Butter
- 2 to 3 tablespoons cold water

Filling

- 2 (4.67-ounce) packages crème de menthe layered mint thins
- ¾ cup sugar
- ¾ cup LAND O LAKES® Butter, softened
- 1 cup real semi-sweet chocolate chips, melted, cooled
- 1 teaspoon vanilla
- ¾ cup pasteurized refrigerated real egg product

• Heat oven to 475°F. Combine flour and salt in large bowl; cut in 6 tablespoons butter with pastry blender or fork until mixture resembles coarse crumbs. Stir in enough water with fork just until flour is moistened. Shape into ball; flatten slightly.

• Roll out ball of dough on lightly floured surface into 12-inch circle. Fold into quarters. Place dough into 9-inch pie pan; unfold, pressing firmly against bottom and sides. Trim crust to ½-inch from edge of pan; crimp or flute edge. Prick bottom and sides of crust with fork. Bake for 8 to 10 minutes or until lightly browned. Cool completely. Set aside.

• Meanwhile, reserve 10 whole mints. Chop remaining mints. Set aside.

• Combine sugar and ¾ cup butter in large bowl. Beat at medium speed, scraping bowl often, until creamy. Add chocolate and vanilla; continue beating until combined. Continue beating, gradually adding real egg product and scraping bowl often, until light and fluffy. Gently stir in chopped mints.

• Spoon mixture into cooled crust. Press whole mints into top of pie. Refrigerate until firm (3 to 4 hours).

tip:

Accurate measurements are the keys to successful pie crust. Too much flour makes a tough pastry, too much butter makes the crust crumbly and too much water makes it tough and soggy.

Peaches & Cream Brownie Mud Pie

Preparation time: **20 minutes** | Baking time: **15 minutes** | **12 servings**

Brownie

½ cup sugar

¼ cup LAND O LAKES® Butter, softened

1 (1-ounce) square unsweetened baking chocolate, melted

1 egg

½ cup all-purpose flour

¼ teaspoon baking powder

Filling

1 cup thick chocolate fudge ice cream topping

1 quart peach ice cream, slightly softened*

Garnish

Thick chocolate fudge ice cream topping, if desired

Fresh peach slices, if desired

• Heat oven to 350°F. Combine sugar and butter in large bowl. Beat at medium speed, scraping bowl often, until creamy. Add chocolate and egg. Continue beating until well mixed. Reduce speed to low; add flour and baking powder. Beat until well mixed.

• Spread batter into greased 9-inch pie pan. Bake for 15 to 18 minutes or until edges just begin to pull away from sides of pan. (DO NOT OVERBAKE.) Cool 1 hour.

• Spread ice cream topping over cooled brownie. Spread softened ice cream over topping. Cover; freeze until firm (4 hours).

• To serve, cut into wedges while frozen. Drizzle each serving with ice cream topping, if desired. Garnish with peach slices, if desired.

*Substitute your favorite flavor ice cream.

Yogurt Berry Pie

Preparation time: **25 minutes** | Baking time: **15 minutes** | **10 servings**

Crust

2   cups vanilla wafer crumbs

¼   cup LAND O LAKES® Butter, melted

Filling

1   pint fresh strawberries, hulled, chopped

⅓   cup sugar

2   (8-ounce) containers vanilla or strawberry-flavored yogurt

1   cup LAND O LAKES™ Heavy Whipping Cream

• Heat oven to 300°F. Combine all crust ingredients in medium bowl. Press mixture evenly onto bottom and up sides of ungreased 9-inch pie pan. Bake for 15 to 20 minutes or until crust is evenly browned. Cool 30 minutes.

• Combine strawberries, sugar and yogurt in medium bowl.

• Beat whipping cream in small bowl at high speed until stiff peaks form (3 to 4 minutes). Gently stir into strawberry mixture. Spoon strawberry mixture into cooled crust. Cover; freeze until firm (8 hours or overnight).

• Remove from freezer 30 minutes before serving. To serve, cut into wedges.

tip:
You can substitute other fruits for the strawberries and use corresponding flavored yogurt in the recipe, such as raspberries and raspberry yogurt, or chopped fresh peaches and peach yogurt.

tip:
If crust sticks to pie pan when removing wedges, place pie pan in a pan of 1-inch deep hot tap water for 30 to 60 seconds or until wedges can be removed easily.

Magic Coconut Custard Pie

Preparation time: **10 minutes** | Baking time: **40 minutes** | 8 servings

    2 cups milk
    1 cup sweetened flaked coconut
    ¾ cup sugar
    ½ cup all-purpose flour
    3 tablespoons LAND O LAKES® Butter, melted
    4 eggs
    1 teaspoon vanilla

       Freshly grated whole nutmeg, if desired
       Cut-up fresh fruit

• Heat oven to 325°F. Grease and flour 9-inch pie pan; set aside.

• Place milk in 5-cup blender container; add all remaining ingredients except nutmeg and fruit. Cover; blend at medium speed until well mixed (1 to 2 minutes).

• Pour egg mixture into prepared pie pan; sprinkle with nutmeg, if desired. Bake for 40 to 50 minutes or until knife inserted in center comes out clean.

• Serve warm or chilled with fresh fruit. Store refrigerated.

S'more Pie

Preparation time: **30 minutes** | Baking time: **4 minutes** | **12 servings**

Crust

1¼ cups (about 18) finely crushed graham crackers

¼ cup sugar

⅓ cup LAND O LAKES® Butter, melted

Filling

⅔ cup LAND O LAKES™ Heavy Whipping Cream

2 (7-ounce) milk chocolate candy bars, broken into pieces

½ teaspoon vanilla

Topping

1⅓ cups LAND O LAKES™ Heavy Whipping Cream

1 cup marshmallow crème

2 (1.55-ounce) milk chocolate candy bars, broken into pieces

• Heat oven to 375°F. Combine all crust ingredients in medium bowl. Press onto bottom of ungreased 9-inch springform or pie pan. Bake for 4 to 5 minutes or until lightly browned. Cool completely.

• Meanwhile, heat ⅔ cup whipping cream in 1-quart saucepan over medium heat, stirring occasionally, until cream just comes to a boil (2 to 3 minutes). Remove from heat. Add all remaining filling ingredients; stir until smooth. Pour over cooled crust. Freeze 30 minutes.

• Combine 1⅓ cups whipping cream and marshmallow crème in large bowl. Beat at high speed until stiff peaks form. Spread over chocolate filling. Garnish with candy bar pieces. Refrigerate at least 4 hours or overnight.

Macadamia Tart

Preparation time: **45 minutes** | Baking time: **42 minutes** | **10 servings**

Pastry

1½ cups all-purpose flour

1 tablespoon sugar

½ cup cold LAND O LAKES® Butter

5 to 6 tablespoons cold water

Filling

1 cup firmly packed brown sugar

1 tablespoon all-purpose flour

1 cup LAND O LAKES™ Heavy Whipping Cream

½ cup coarsely chopped macadamia nuts

Drizzle

2 tablespoons real semi-sweet chocolate chips

½ teaspoon shortening

Macadamia nuts, if desired

• Heat oven to 375°F. Combine 1½ cups flour and sugar in medium bowl; cut in butter with pastry blender or fork until mixture resembles coarse crumbs. Stir in enough cold water just until flour is moistened. Shape into a ball.

• Roll pastry ball into 13-inch circle on lightly floured surface. Place into ungreased 11-inch tart pan with removable bottom. Press pastry onto bottom and up sides of pan; cut away excess pastry. Bake for 17 to 20 minutes or until pastry is very lightly browned.

• Combine brown sugar and 1 tablespoon flour in medium bowl until well mixed. Gradually stir in whipping cream. Pour into hot, partially baked crust; sprinkle with ½ cup macadamia nuts. Bake for 25 to 30 minutes or until filling is bubbly all over. Cool completely (2 hours).

• Melt chocolate chips and shortening in 1-quart saucepan over low heat, stirring constantly, until smooth (1 to 2 minutes). Drizzle over tart. Garnish with macadamia nuts, if desired. Refrigerate at least 1 hour. Let stand 15 minutes before serving.

tip:

If using a smaller tart pan, fill only to ¼-inch from top of tart shell.

tip :

If using nonstick tart pan, decrease final baking time to 20 to 25 minutes.

Holiday
Shortbread
Tidbits, p. 121

Easy Gingerbread
Cutouts
(opposite page), p. 126

HOLIDAY
BAKING

Nothing says "Happy Holidays" like a bundle of home-baked goodies. Check out this special collection of recipes for everything you need to make this festive season merry and bright.

Gingered Crème Brûlée

Preparation time: **30 minutes** | Baking time: **1 hour** | **8 servings**

Custard

1 cup LAND O LAKES™ Half & Half

2 cups LAND O LAKES™ Heavy Whipping Cream

1 (1-ounce) piece fresh gingerroot, peeled, cut into 8 pieces

½ cup sugar

4 eggs

Topping

4 teaspoons sugar

• Heat oven to 250°F. Pour half & half, whipping cream and ginger into heavy 2-quart saucepan. Cook over low heat for 30 minutes. Remove ginger.

• Beat ½ cup sugar and eggs in medium bowl until sugar dissolves and mixture is slightly thickened. Slowly add whipping cream mixture, mixing well after each addition.

• Place eight (4-ounce) ungreased ramekins or custard cups into large baking pan. Divide mixture evenly among ramekins. Place baking pan on oven rack; pour boiling water into baking pan to ½-inch depth. Bake for 1 to 1½ hours or until custards are just set around edges. Remove from water; cool to room temperature. Cover; refrigerate until thoroughly chilled (8 hours or overnight).

• Heat broiler. Just before serving, sprinkle top of each custard evenly with ½ teaspoon sugar. Place ramekins on baking pan. Broil 3 to 4 inches from heat just until sugar caramelizes (1 to 2 minutes). Serve immediately.

tip:

Baking time varies with the type of custard cups used and with the heat of the water bath. With metal, thin porcelain and glass dishes, cooking time is less. Heavy pottery dishes take more time to conduct heat. Custard cups that are deep with less surface area take more time than cups that are shallow with more surface.

Holiday Shortbread Tidbits

Preparation time: **20 minutes** | Baking time: **14 minutes per pan** | **256 tidbits**

- ½ cup LAND O LAKES® Butter, softened
- ¼ cup sugar
- ¼ teaspoon almond extract
- 1¼ cups all-purpose flour
- ¼ teaspoon salt
- 4 teaspoons multi-colored nonpareils

• Heat oven to 325°F. Line 8-inch square baking pan with plastic food wrap, leaving 1-inch overhang. Set aside.

• Combine butter, sugar and almond extract in medium bowl. Beat at medium speed, scraping bowl often, until creamy. Reduce speed to low; add flour and salt. Beat until well mixed. Stir in nonpareils.

• Knead mixture 4 to 5 times in bowl until dough forms a ball. Pat dough evenly into prepared pan. Use plastic wrap to lift dough from pan. Cut dough into ½-inch squares. Gently place squares ½-inch apart onto ungreased cookie sheets; discard plastic wrap. Bake for 14 to 16 minutes or until bottoms just begin to brown.

tip:

Avoid last minute holiday hassle—make these sweet tidbits before the holiday season. Store between sheets of waxed paper in container with tight-fitting lid; freeze for up to 2 months.

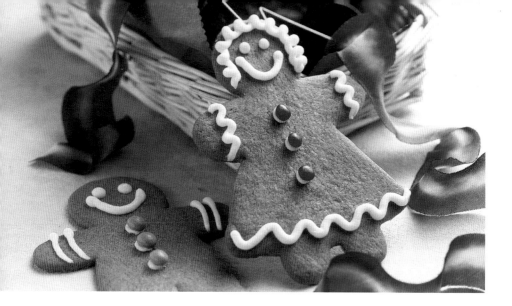

Holiday Ginger Cookies

Preparation time: **1 hour** | Baking time: **6 minutes per pan** | **2 dozen cookies**

Cookie

- 1¼ cups sugar
- 1 cup LAND O LAKES® Butter, softened
- 1 egg
- 3 tablespoons molasses
- 1 teaspoon vanilla
- 3 cups all-purpose flour
- 2 teaspoons ground cinnamon
- 1 teaspoon ground ginger
- ½ teaspoon baking soda
- ¼ teaspoon salt

Frosting

- 3 cups powdered sugar
- ⅓ cup LAND O LAKES® Butter, softened
- 1 teaspoon vanilla
- 1 to 2 tablespoons milk

• Combine sugar, butter, egg, molasses and vanilla in large bowl. Beat at medium speed, scraping bowl often, until creamy. Reduce speed to low; add all remaining cookie ingredients. Beat until well mixed. Divide dough in half; wrap in plastic food wrap. Refrigerate until firm (1 to 2 hours).

• Heat oven to 375°F. Roll out dough on lightly floured surface, one-half at a time (keeping remaining dough refrigerated), to ⅛-inch thickness. Cut with 4-inch cookie cutter. Place cookies 1 inch apart onto ungreased cookie sheets. Bake for 6 to 9 minutes or until set. Let stand 1 minute; remove from cookie sheets. Cool completely.

• Combine powdered sugar, ⅓ cup butter and 1 teaspoon vanilla in small bowl. Beat at low speed, adding enough milk for desired spreading consistency. Decorate cooled cookies with frosting as desired.

English Toffee

Preparation time: **15 minutes** | Cooking time: **25 minutes** | 1¼ **pounds**

    1 cup LAND O LAKES® Butter (no substitutions)

    1 cup sugar

    1 cup real semi-sweet chocolate chips

    ¼ cup chopped pecans

• Combine butter and sugar in heavy 2-quart saucepan. Cook over medium heat, stirring occasionally with a wooden spoon, until candy thermometer reaches 300°F. or small amount of mixture dropped into ice water forms brittle strands (25 to 30 minutes).

• Quickly spread into 15×10×1-inch jelly-roll pan. Sprinkle chocolate chips over hot candy; let stand 5 minutes. Spread melted chocolate evenly over candy; sprinkle with pecans. Cool completely; break into pieces.

tip:
To prevent toffee mixture from separating, stir occasionally and gently with a wooden spoon until mixture reaches 260°F. to 265°F. Continue cooking, stirring as few times as possible, until mixture reaches 300°F. Stirring too much contributes to toffee separating. It is important to keep the mixture from burning, so stir gently occasionally.

tip:
Store butter toffee in a cool, dry place in container with tight-fitting lid. Do not refrigerate.

Peppermint Twists

Preparation time: **1 hour** | Baking time: **11 minutes per pan** | 28 cookies

½ cup LAND O LAKES® Butter, softened

⅓ cup sugar

1 egg yolk

¾ teaspoon peppermint extract

½ teaspoon vanilla

1¼ cups all-purpose flour

¼ teaspoon salt

8 to 10 drops red food color

Coarse grain sugar, if desired

28 milk chocolate candy kisses

• Heat oven to 350°F. Place butter, sugar, egg yolk, peppermint extract and vanilla in large bowl. Beat at medium speed, scraping bowl often, until creamy. Reduce speed to low; add flour and salt. Beat until well mixed.

• Remove half of dough from bowl. Add small amount of red food color to dough in bowl; mix well.

• Divide each half of dough into quarters; roll each quarter to 7-inch log. Place 1 red log next to 1 white log; twist gently to swirl dough. Roll gently to smooth. Repeat with remaining dough.

• Cut each swirled rope of dough into 7 pieces; roll each piece gently into a ball. Roll each ball in coarse grain sugar, if desired. Place onto ungreased cookie sheets. Bake for 11 to 13 minutes or until edges are lightly browned. Immediately press 1 chocolate star in center of each ball.

Cashew Butter Crunch

Preparation time: **10 minutes** | Cooking time: **33 minutes** | 1¼ pounds (2 dozen pieces)

- 1 cup sugar
- 1 cup LAND O LAKES® Butter (no substitutions)
- 1 tablespoon light corn syrup
- 1½ cups salted cashew pieces*

• Combine sugar, butter and corn syrup in heavy 2-quart saucepan. Cook over medium-low heat, stirring occasionally, until butter is melted and mixture comes to a boil (8 to 10 minutes). Continue cooking, stirring occasionally, until candy thermometer reaches 290°F. or small amount of mixture dropped into ice water forms brittle strands (25 to 30 minutes). Remove from heat; stir in cashews.

• Spread to ¼-inch thickness on buttered 15×10×1-inch jelly-roll pan. Cool completely; break into pieces.

*Substitute 1½ cups of your favorite salted nuts.

Easy Gingerbread Cut-Outs

Preparation time: **35 minutes** | Baking time: **7 minutes per pan** | **2 dozen cookies**

Cookie

- 1 (18.25-ounce) package spice cake mix*
- ¾ cup LAND O LAKES® Butter, softened
- 1 egg
- 2 tablespoons orange juice or milk
- 1 teaspoon ground cinnamon
- 1 teaspoon vanilla
- ½ teaspoon ground ginger

Frosting

- 4½ cups powdered sugar
- ⅓ cup LAND O LAKES® Butter, softened
- 2 tablespoons orange juice or milk
- 2 to 3 tablespoons milk
- Food color, if desired

• Combine half of cake mix and all remaining cookie ingredients in large bowl. Beat at low speed, scraping bowl often, until well mixed. Add remaining cake mix; continue beating until well mixed. Divide dough in half; wrap each in plastic food wrap. Refrigerate until firm (at least 2 hours or overnight).

• Heat oven to 375°F. Roll out dough on lightly floured surface, one-half at a time (keeping remaining dough refrigerated), to ⅛-inch thickness. Cut with 3 to 4-inch cookie cutter. Place 2 inches apart onto ungreased cookie sheets. Bake for 7 to 9 minutes or until set. Let stand 1 minute; remove from cookie sheets. Cool completely.

• Combine all frosting ingredients except milk and food color in large bowl. Beat at low speed, scraping bowl often and gradually adding enough milk for desired spreading consistency. Tint with food color, if desired. Frost cooled cookies. Decorate as desired.

*Substitute 1 (18.25-ounce) package carrot cake mix.

tip:

The holidays are the time to decorate even ordinary cookies to make them extraordinary. For simple decorations, pipe frosting using a disposable pastry bag and decorating tips. Start with just two tips—star and writing. They'll yield an endless array of cookie decorations.

Caramel Apple Crisp

Preparation time: **15 minutes** | Baking time: **20 minutes** | **4 servings**

Filling

¼ cup LAND O LAKES® Butter, melted

⅓ cup firmly packed brown sugar

1 (21-ounce) can apple pie filling

Topping

⅓ cup graham cracker crumbs

¼ cup uncooked quick-cooking oats

2 tablespoons firmly packed brown sugar

2 tablespoons LAND O LAKES® Butter, melted

LAND O LAKES™ Fat Free Half & Half or Half & Half, if desired

• Heat oven to 375°F. Combine all filling ingredients in ungreased 1-quart casserole; mix well.

• Combine all topping ingredients in small bowl; mix well. Sprinkle topping over apple mixture. Bake for 20 to 25 minutes or until topping is lightly browned.

• To serve, spoon into individual serving dishes. Serve with half & half, if desired.

tip:
To make ahead, prepare recipe as directed above. Cover unbaked crisp with aluminum foil; freeze. To serve, uncover; bake as directed above increasing baking time to 25 to 30 minutes.

Almond Strips

Preparation time: **1 hour** | Baking time: **14 minutes per pan** | **5½ dozen cookies**

Filling

⅓ cup firmly packed brown sugar

1 (8-ounce) can almond paste*

1 egg white

Pastry

3 cups all-purpose flour

¼ cup sugar

¼ teaspoon salt

1½ cups cold LAND O LAKES®
    Butter

5 to 6 tablespoons cold water

Glaze

1 cup powdered sugar

¼ teaspoon almond extract

2 to 3 tablespoons milk

Decorator sugar, if desired

• Heat oven to 375°F. Combine all filling ingredients in small bowl with fork until well mixed.

• Combine flour, sugar and salt in large bowl; cut in butter with pastry blender or fork until mixture resembles coarse crumbs. Mix in enough water until flour is just moistened.

• Shape dough into ball; divide into fourths. Roll out dough, one-fourth at a time (keeping remaining dough refrigerated), on lightly floured surface to 12×8-inch rectangle. Cut into 4 (8×3-inch) strips.

• Place strips onto ungreased cookie sheets. Spread about 1 tablespoon filling down center of each strip. Moisten edges of strips with water. Fold pastry over filling; press edges together with fork. Prick tops in several places. Bake for 14 to 17 minutes or until golden brown. Let stand 2 to 3 minutes; remove from cookie sheets. Cool completely. Repeat with remaining pastry and filling.

• Combine powdered sugar, almond extract and enough milk for desired glazing consistency. Drizzle glaze over cooled cookie strips. Sprinkle with decorator sugar, if desired. Cut strips into 2-inch lengths.

*Substitute 1 (7-ounce) roll almond paste.

tip:
Almond paste, in cans or tubes, is typically found near the pie filling at your grocery store.

Eggnog Glazed Spritz Cookies

Preparation time: **45 minutes** | Baking time: **6 minutes per pan** | **4 dozen cookies**

Cookie

- 1 cup LAND O LAKES® Butter, softened
- ⅔ cup sugar
- 1 egg
- 1 tablespoon vanilla
- 2¼ cups all-purpose flour
- 1 teaspoon ground nutmeg

Glaze

- 1 cup powdered sugar
- ¼ cup LAND O LAKES® Butter, melted
- ¼ teaspoon rum extract
- 1 to 2 tablespoons hot water

  Multi-colored decorator candies, if desired

• Heat oven to 375°F. Combine 1 cup butter, sugar, egg and vanilla in large bowl. Beat at medium speed, scraping bowl often, until creamy. Reduce speed to low; add flour and nutmeg. Beat until well mixed.

• Fit cookie press with template; fill with dough. Press dough 1 inch apart onto ungreased cookie sheets. Bake for 6 to 10 minutes or until edges are very lightly browned.

• Stir together powdered sugar, ¼ cup butter, rum extract and enough hot water for desired glazing consistency in small bowl. While still warm, brush top of cookies with glaze; sprinkle with candies, if desired.

Melt-In-Your-Mouth Truffles

Preparation time: **30 minutes** | **36 truffles**

½ cup LAND O LAKES™ Heavy Whipping Cream

8 ounces dark sweet chocolate, coarsely chopped*

¼ cup LAND O LAKES® Butter, softened

2 teaspoons vanilla**

Finely chopped nuts, if desired

Unsweetened cocoa, if desired

Powdered sugar, if desired

• Combine whipping cream and chocolate in 2-quart saucepan. Cook over low heat, stirring constantly, until chocolate is melted and mixture is smooth (2 to 4 minutes). Stir in butter until melted. Cool to room temperature (about 30 minutes). Stir in vanilla. Cover; refrigerate until firm enough to shape (at least 8 hours).

• To make truffles, shape about 1 teaspoon cold chocolate mixture into 1-inch balls. (Mixture will be soft. Do not overwork.) Roll in finely chopped nuts, cocoa or powdered sugar, if desired. Place onto parchment-lined baking sheet. Refrigerate until firm (at least 2 hours). Cover; store refrigerated.

*Substitute 8 (1-ounce) squares semi-sweet chocolate, coarsely chopped.

**Substitute ½ teaspoon mint extract or 4 teaspoons your favorite liqueur.

microwave directions:

Place whipping cream and chocolate in 2-cup measure. Microwave on HIGH, stirring after half the time, until chocolate is melted (1 to 2 minutes). Stir until smooth; stir in butter until melted. Cool to room temperature (about 30 minutes). Stir in vanilla. Cover; refrigerate until firm enough to shape (at least 8 hours). To make truffles, follow shaping directions above. Refrigerate until firm (at least 2 hours).

tip:

Chocolate mixture can be kept in refrigerator for up to 3 days before forming into balls.

Christmas Noodle Trees

Preparation time: **20 minutes** | Cooking time: **4 minutes** | **15 trees**

¼ cup LAND O LAKES® Butter

1 (10½-ounce) package (4 cups) miniature marshmallows

3 tablespoons creamy peanut butter

1 teaspoon vanilla

½ teaspoon green food color

1 (6-ounce) package (4 cups) chow mein noodles*

1 tablespoon red cinnamon candies

8 small gumdrops, halved**

• Combine butter and marshmallows in 3-quart saucepan. Cook over low heat, stirring constantly, until smooth (4 to 6 minutes). Stir in peanut butter, vanilla and food color; mix well. Add noodles; quickly stir until well coated.

• Lightly spray a tablespoon with no-stick cooking spray. Drop heaping tablespoonfuls of mixture onto waxed paper. Shape mixture into trees with lightly greased fingers, working quickly so mixture does not harden.

• Immediately decorate trees with candies using gumdrop halves for trunk. Let stand until firm (about 30 minutes). Store in loosely covered container between sheets of waxed paper.

*Substitute 4 cups rice noodles.

**Substitute 15 pretzel nuggets.

tip:
If cinnamon candies do not stick, use a dab of honey or light corn syrup as glue.

tip:
Gift idea: Wrap trees in colored plastic food wrap and tie with a ribbon.

Carrot Cake with Cream Cheese Frosting, p. 144

Creamy Lemon Meringue Pie *(opposite page)*, p. 145

FAMILY
FAVORITES

At our house, family time means meal time, so we're always on the lookout for recipes like these: easy to prepare and satisfying to eat. They're among our favorite recipes, and we're sure they'll soon be among yours, as well.

Cinnamon Raisin Bread Pudding with Maple Sauce

Preparation time: **15 minutes** | Baking time: **40 minutes** | **6 servings**

Pudding

- ¼ cup LAND O LAKES® Butter
- 8 slices (4 cups) cinnamon raisin bread, cut into 1-inch cubes
- 2 cups milk
- ½ cup sugar
- 2 eggs, slightly beaten
- 1 teaspoon vanilla
- ½ teaspoon ground cinnamon

Sauce

- ½ cup firmly packed brown sugar
- ¼ cup LAND O LAKES® Butter
- ½ cup maple syrup
- 2 tablespoons LAND O LAKES™ Fat Free Half & Half or Half & Half

• Heat oven to 350°F. Place ¼ cup butter in 1½-quart casserole; melt butter in oven (about 5 minutes). Add bread cubes; toss to coat.

• Combine milk, sugar, eggs, vanilla and cinnamon in medium bowl; stir to blend. Pour over bread cubes. Bake for 40 to 45 minutes or until center is set.

• Meanwhile, combine all sauce ingredients in 1-quart saucepan. Cook over medium heat, stirring occasionally, until mixture comes to a boil (5 minutes). Continue cooking until mixture is thickened (3 to 4 minutes).

• Serve warm sauce over warm bread pudding.

Gingersnaps

Preparation time: **45 minutes** | Baking time: **8 minutes per pan** | **5 dozen cookies**

1¼ cups sugar -divided

¾ cup LAND O LAKES® Butter, softened

⅓ cup molasses

1 egg

2¼ cups all-purpose flour

2 teaspoons baking soda

1 teaspoon ground cinnamon

1 teaspoon ground ginger

• Combine 1 cup sugar and butter in large bowl. Beat at medium speed, scraping bowl often, until creamy. Add molasses and egg; continue beating until well mixed. Reduce speed to low; add flour, baking soda, cinnamon and ginger. Beat until well mixed. Cover; refrigerate 30 minutes.

• Heat oven to 350°F. Shape dough into 1-inch balls. Roll balls in remaining ¼ cup sugar. Place 2 inches apart onto ungreased cookie sheets. Bake for 8 to 11 minutes or until set and lightly browned.

Risotto Rice Pudding

Preparation time: **5 minutes** | Cooking time: **24 minutes** | **8 (½-cup) servings**

1 cup water	1 teaspoon freshly grated lemon peel
1 cup Arborio rice	¼ to ½ teaspoon ground cinnamon, if desired
¼ cup LAND O LAKES® Butter	
2½ cups hot milk	½ cup LAND O LAKES® Sour Cream
⅓ cup sugar	
¼ cup raisins	Lemon twists, if desired
1 teaspoon vanilla	

• Bring water to a boil in 3-quart saucepan over medium-high heat (5 to 6 minutes). Add rice and butter; continue cooking until mixture returns to a boil (1 to 2 minutes). Reduce heat to low. Cover; cook until liquid is absorbed (8 to 10 minutes).

• Add hot milk and sugar. Cook over medium heat, stirring occasionally, until rice is creamy and tender (10 to 12 minutes). Add raisins, vanilla, lemon peel and cinnamon, if desired, during last few minutes of cooking time. Remove pan from heat; stir in sour cream.

• To serve, divide mixture evenly among 8 individual dessert dishes. Serve warm, at room temperature or chilled. Garnish with lemon twists, if desired.

Southern Berry Cobbler

Preparation time: **30 minutes** | Baking time: **25 minutes** | 8 servings

Filling

1½ cups sugar

2 (6-ounce) packages fresh
blackberries*

2 (6-ounce) packages fresh
raspberries**

¼ cup cornstarch

2 teaspoons lemon juice

1 teaspoon ground cinnamon

Topping

2 cups all-purpose baking mix

⅔ cup milk

¼ cup LAND O LAKES® Butter,
melted

2 tablespoons sugar, divided

LAND O LAKES™ Heavy
Whipping Cream, whipped,
sweetened, if desired

• Heat oven to 400°F. Combine all filling ingredients in 3-quart saucepan. Cook over medium-high heat, stirring constantly, until mixture comes to a full boil (10 to 12 minutes). Continue boiling 1 minute. Remove from heat. Cover; keep hot.

• Immediately, combine baking mix, milk, butter and 1 tablespoon sugar in medium bowl. Pour hot berry mixture into ungreased 2-quart casserole. Drop 8 equal portions of topping onto hot filling. Sprinkle with remaining sugar.

• Bake for 25 to 30 minutes or until topping is golden brown and filling is bubbly around edges. Serve warm with sweetened whipped cream, if desired.

*Substitute 1 (14-ounce) package frozen blackberries, thawed.

**Substitute 1 (14-ounce) package frozen raspberries, thawed.

Carrot Cake with Cream Cheese Frosting *(photo on page 138)*

Preparation time: **25 minutes** | Baking time: **40 minutes** | **15 servings**

Cake

- 1 cup LAND O LAKES® Butter, melted
- 1 cup firmly packed brown sugar
- ¾ cup sugar
- 3 eggs
- 1 (11-ounce) can mandarin orange segments, undrained
- 2½ teaspoons vanilla
- 2 teaspoons freshly grated orange peel
- 2¾ cups all-purpose flour
- 1 tablespoon ground cinnamon
- 2 teaspoons baking soda
- ½ teaspoon salt
- ¾ cup sweetened flaked coconut
- ½ cup chopped pecans
- 4 medium (2 cups) carrots, grated

Frosting

- 3½ cups powdered sugar
- 1 (8-ounce) package cream cheese, softened
- 2 tablespoons LAND O LAKES® Butter, softened
- 2 teaspoons vanilla
- Chopped pecans

• Heat oven to 350°F. Grease and flour 13×9-inch baking pan. Set aside.

• Combine 1 cup butter, brown sugar, sugar and eggs in large bowl. Beat at medium speed, scraping bowl often, until creamy. Add mandarin orange segments, 2½ teaspoons vanilla and orange peel; continue beating until well mixed. Reduce speed to low; add flour, cinnamon, baking soda and salt. Beat, scraping bowl often, until well mixed. Stir in coconut, ½ cup pecans and carrots by hand.

• Pour batter into prepared pan. Bake for 40 to 50 minutes or until toothpick inserted in center comes out clean. Cool completely.

• Combine all frosting ingredients except chopped pecans in small bowl. Beat at medium speed, scraping bowl often, until smooth. Frost cooled cake; sprinkle with pecans.

Creamy Lemon Meringue Pie *(photo on page 139)*

Preparation time: **1 hour** | Baking time: **18 minutes** | **8 servings**

Crust

- 1 cup all-purpose flour
- ⅛ teaspoon salt
- 6 tablespoons cold LAND O LAKES® Butter
- 2 to 3 tablespoons cold water

Filling

- 1¼ cups sugar
- ⅓ cup cornstarch
- ¼ teaspoon salt
- 1¼ cups water

- 4 egg yolks, beaten
- ½ cup fresh lemon juice
- 3 tablespoons LAND O LAKES® Butter
- 2 teaspoons freshly grated lemon peel

Meringue

- 4 egg whites
- ½ teaspoon cream of tartar
- ½ cup sugar

• Heat oven to 475°F. Combine flour and salt in large bowl; cut in butter with pastry blender or fork until mixture resembles coarse crumbs. Stir in water with fork just until flour is moistened. Shape dough into ball; flatten slightly.

• Roll out dough on lightly floured surface into 12-inch circle. Fold into quarters. Place dough into 9-inch pie pan; unfold, pressing firmly against bottom and sides. Trim crust to ½ inch from edge of pan; crimp or flute edge. Prick bottom and sides of crust with fork. Bake for 8 to 10 minutes or until lightly browned. Cool completely.

• Reduce oven temperature to 325°F. Meanwhile, combine 1¼ cups sugar, cornstarch and salt in 2-quart saucepan. Gradually stir in 1¼ cups water. Cook over medium heat, stirring constantly, until mixture comes to a full boil (7 to 9 minutes). Boil 1 minute. Gradually stir ½ cup hot mixture into beaten egg yolks with wire whisk. Gradually stir egg mixture into remaining hot mixture. Continue cooking, stirring constantly, until mixture reaches 160°F. and is thickened (2 to 3 minutes). Whisk in lemon juice, butter and lemon peel. Remove from heat; set aside.

• Beat egg whites and cream of tartar in large bowl at high speed until foamy. Continue beating, gradually adding ½ cup sugar, until stiff peaks form and mixture is glossy (3 to 4 minutes). Pour hot filling into baked pie shell. Spread meringue over hot filling, completely sealing to edge of crust and mounding slightly in center.

• Bake for 25 to 30 minutes or until meringue reaches 160°F and is lightly browned. Cool at room temperature 2 hours. Refrigerate at least 1 hour before serving. Store refrigerated.

tip:

For a Lime Meringue Pie, substitute fresh lime juice for fresh lemon juice and freshly grated lime peel for freshly grated lemon peel.

Granny's Peaches & Cream Cobbler

Preparation time: **30 minutes** | Baking time: **40 minutes** | 8 servings

Filling

- 1 cup sugar
- 2 eggs, slightly beaten
- 2 tablespoons all-purpose flour
- ½ teaspoon ground nutmeg
- 2 (16-ounce) packages sliced frozen peaches, thawed, drained*

Topping

- 1½ cups all-purpose flour
- 5 tablespoons sugar, divided
- 1 teaspoon baking powder
- ½ teaspoon salt
- ⅓ cup cold LAND O LAKES® Butter
- 1 egg, slightly beaten
- 3 tablespoons milk

LAND O LAKES™ Heavy Whipping Cream, if desired

• Heat oven to 400°F. Combine all filling ingredients except peaches in large bowl. Stir in peaches. Spoon into ungreased 13×9-inch baking pan.

• Combine flour, 2 tablespoons sugar, baking powder and salt in medium bowl; cut in butter with pastry blender or fork until mixture resembles coarse crumbs. Stir in egg and milk just until moistened. Crumble mixture over peaches; sprinkle with remaining sugar.

• Bake for 40 to 45 minutes or until golden brown and bubbly around edges.

• To serve, spoon cobbler into individual dessert dishes. Top with whipping cream, if desired.

*Substitute 4 to 6 medium (4 cups) peaches, peeled, sliced.

Mom's Butter Cookies

Preparation time: **45 minutes** | Baking time: **8 minutes per pan** | 3 dozen cookies

- 1 cup LAND O LAKES® Butter, softened
- ½ cup firmly packed brown sugar
- ¼ cup sugar
- 2 cups all-purpose flour

• Combine all ingredients except flour in large bowl. Beat at medium speed until creamy. Reduce speed to low; add flour. Beat until well mixed.

• Divide dough in half. Wrap each half in plastic food wrap; flatten slightly. Refrigerate until firm (30 minutes or overnight).

• Heat oven to 350°F. Roll out dough on lightly floured surface, one-half at a time (keeping remaining dough refrigerated), to ⅛-inch thickness. Cut with 3-inch cookie cutters. Place 1 inch apart onto ungreased cookie sheets. Bake for 8 to 10 minutes or until edges are very lightly browned. Cool 1 minute; remove from cookie sheet.

Blue Ribbon Apple Pie

Preparation time: **1 hour** | Baking time: **45 minutes** | **8 servings**

Crust

- 2 cups all-purpose flour
- 1 teaspoon sugar
- ¼ teaspoon salt
- ¼ teaspoon ground cinnamon
- ¼ teaspoon ground nutmeg
- ⅔ cup cold LAND O LAKES® Butter
- 4 to 5 tablespoons cold water

Filling

- ½ cup sugar
- ¼ cup firmly packed brown sugar
- ¼ cup all-purpose flour
- ½ teaspoon ground cinnamon
- ½ teaspoon ground nutmeg
- 6 medium (6 cups) tart cooking apples, peeled, sliced ¼-inch

Topping

- 1 tablespoon LAND O LAKES® Butter, melted
- 1 teaspoon sugar

• Heat oven to 400°F. Combine 2 cups flour, 1 teaspoon sugar, salt, ¼ teaspoon cinnamon and ¼ teaspoon nutmeg in large bowl. Cut in ⅔ cup butter with pastry blender or fork until mixture resembles coarse crumbs. Stir in enough water with fork just until moistened.

• Divide dough in half; shape each half into a ball. Flatten slightly. Wrap 1 ball in plastic food wrap; refrigerate. Roll remaining ball of dough on lightly floured surface into 12-inch circle. Fold into quarters. Place dough into 9-inch pie pan; unfold dough, pressing firmly against bottom and sides. Trim crust to ½ inch from rim of pan; set aside.

• Combine all filling ingredients except apples in large bowl. Add apples; toss lightly to coat.

• Spoon apple mixture into prepared crust. Roll remaining ball of dough into 12-inch circle. Fold into quarters. Place dough over filling; unfold. Trim, seal and crimp or flute edge. Cut 5 or 6 large slits in top crust. Brush top with 1 tablespoon melted butter; sprinkle with 1 teaspoon sugar. Cover edge of crust with 2-inch strip of aluminum foil.

• Bake for 35 minutes; remove aluminum foil. Continue baking for 10 to 20 minutes or until crust is lightly browned and juice begins to bubble through slits in crust. Cool pie 1 hour; serve warm. Store refrigerated.

tip:

If desired, remove pie from oven when lightly browned and bubbly. Run knife through slits in crust. Pour ½ cup whipping cream evenly through all slits. Return to oven for 5 minutes to warm whipping cream.

Old-Fashioned Bread Pudding with Vanilla Sauce

Preparation time: **15 minutes** | Baking time: **40 minutes** | **8 servings, 1½ cups sauce**

Pudding

- 4 cups (8 slices) cubed white bread
- ½ cup raisins
- 2 cups milk
- ¼ cup LAND O LAKES® Butter
- ½ cup sugar
- 2 eggs, slightly beaten
- 1 teaspoon vanilla
- ½ teaspoon ground nutmeg

Sauce

- ½ cup LAND O LAKES® Butter
- ½ cup sugar
- ½ cup firmly packed brown sugar
- ½ cup LAND O LAKES™ Heavy Whipping Cream
- 1 teaspoon vanilla

• Heat oven to 350°F. Combine bread and raisins in large bowl. Combine milk and ¼ cup butter in 1-quart saucepan. Cook over medium heat until butter is melted (4 to 7 minutes). Pour milk mixture over bread; let stand 10 minutes.

• Stir in all remaining pudding ingredients. Pour into greased 1½-quart casserole. Bake for 40 to 50 minutes or until center is set.

• Combine all sauce ingredients except vanilla in 1-quart saucepan. Cook over medium heat, stirring occasionally, until mixture thickens and comes to a full boil (5 to 8 minutes). Stir in vanilla.

• To serve, spoon warm pudding into individual dessert dishes; serve with sauce. Store refrigerated.

Best Ever Oatmeal Cookies

Preparation time: **45 minutes** | Baking time: **8 minutes per pan** | **4 dozen cookies**

3 cups uncooked quick-cooking oats

2 cups firmly packed brown sugar

1 cup LAND O LAKES® Butter, softened

2 eggs

1 teaspoon baking soda

2 teaspoons vanilla

½ teaspoon salt

1½ cups all-purpose flour

• Heat oven to 375°F. Combine all ingredients except flour in large bowl. Beat at low speed, scraping bowl often, until well mixed. Stir in flour by hand.

• Drop dough by rounded tablespoonfuls, 2 inches apart, onto lightly greased cookie sheets. Bake for 8 to 12 minutes or until edges are lightly browned. Let stand 1 minute; remove from cookie sheets.

variation:

Chocolate Drizzled Oatmeal Cookies: Prepare and bake cookies as directed above. Melt ½ cup real semi-sweet or milk chocolate chips and 1 tablespoon shortening. Drizzle mixture over cooled cookies.

tip:

Stir in 1 cup of the following ingredients: mini real semi-sweet chocolate chips, raisins, chopped mixed dried fruit, sweetened flaked coconut or chopped pecans. Bake as directed above.

tip:

Dough is best when baked the day it is made. If dough is stored in the refrigerator, the oats absorb liquid and cause the cookies to be dry.

Four Citrus Pound Cake

Preparation time: **35 minutes** | Baking time: **45 minutes** | **16 servings**

Cake

- 1 grapefruit
- 1 lemon
- 1 lime
- 1 orange
- ½ cup milk
- 1 tablespoon grapefruit juice
- 1¼ cups LAND O LAKES® Butter, softened
- 1½ cups sugar
- 3 eggs
- 2½ cups cake flour*
- 3 tablespoons poppy seed
- ¾ teaspoon baking powder
- ½ teaspoon baking soda
- ¼ teaspoon salt

Glaze

- 2 tablespoons LAND O LAKES® Butter, melted
- 1 tablespoon reserved grapefruit juice
- ¾ cup powdered sugar

  Grated grapefruit, lemon, lime and/or orange peel, if desired

• Heat oven to 350°F. Grease and flour 9- to 12-cup Bundt® pan or 10-inch angel food cake (tube) pan. Set aside.

• Grate peel from grapefruit, lemon, lime and orange. Place 2 teaspoons each grapefruit, lemon, lime and orange peel in small bowl; add milk and 1 tablespoon grapefruit juice. Mix well.

• Combine butter and sugar in large bowl. Beat at medium speed, scraping bowl occasionally, until creamy. Add eggs, one at a time, beating well after each addition. (Mixture will appear curdled.)

• Stir together flour, poppy seed, baking powder, baking soda and salt in another small bowl. Reduce speed to low. Gradually add flour mixture, alternately with milk mixture, beating just until moistened after each addition.

• Spread batter evenly into prepared pan. Bake for 45 to 50 minutes or until toothpick inserted in center comes out clean. Cool pan on wire rack 10 minutes. Remove from pan. Cool completely.

• Combine 2 tablespoons melted butter and 1 tablespoon grapefruit juice in small bowl. Add powdered sugar; stir until well mixed. (Add 1 to 2 tablespoons additional grapefruit juice, if necessary, to reach desired glazing consistency.) Drizzle over cooled cake. Sprinkle with grated peel, if desired.

*Substitute 2¼ cups all-purpose flour.

Chocolate Cake with Peanut Butter Frosting

Preparation time: **35 minutes** | Baking time: **30 minutes** | **12 servings**

Cake

1⅔ cups sugar

¾ cup LAND O LAKES® Butter, softened

3 eggs

1 teaspoon vanilla

2 cups all-purpose flour

⅔ cup unsweetened cocoa

1¼ teaspoons baking soda

½ teaspoon baking powder

½ teaspoon salt

1⅓ cups milk

Frosting

1 cup creamy peanut butter

½ cup LAND O LAKES® Butter, softened

2 cups powdered sugar, sifted

2 teaspoons vanilla

3 to 4 tablespoons milk

• Heat oven to 350°F. Grease and lightly flour 2 (8- or 9-inch) square or round cake pans.

• Combine sugar and ¾ cup butter in large bowl. Beat at medium speed, scraping bowl often, until creamy. Add eggs and 1 teaspoon vanilla; continue beating until well mixed. Add flour, cocoa, baking soda, baking powder and salt to butter mixture alternately with 1⅓ cups milk, beating just until blended.

• Pour batter evenly into prepared pans. Bake for 30 to 40 minutes or until toothpick inserted in center comes out clean. Cool 10 minutes. Remove from pans. Cool completely.

• Meanwhile, place peanut butter and ½ cup butter in small bowl. Beat at low speed, scraping bowl often, until creamy. Add powdered sugar, 2 teaspoons vanilla and enough milk for desired frosting consistency.

• To assemble cake, place 1 cake layer onto serving plate. Spread 1 cup frosting over top; top with second cake layer. Spread remaining frosting over top and sides of cake.

tip:

Make cake and frost the day before. Cover with plastic food wrap or store in container with tight-fitting lid.

index